# 101 Devotionals with Children

# 101 Devotionals with Children

## June Galle Krehbiel

Herald
Press

Scottdale, Pennsylvania
Waterloo, Ontario

**Library of Congress Cataloging-in-Publication Data**
Krehbiel, June Galle, 1949-
   101 devotionals with children / June Galle Krehbiel.
      p.   cm.
   Includes bibliographical references and index.
   ISBN 0-8361-9117-X  (alk. paper)
   1. Childern Prayer—books and devotions—English. I. Title.
II. Title: One hundred and one devotionals with children.
III. Title: One hundred and one devotionals with children.
BV4870.K685   1999
249—dc21                                        99-30151

The paper used in this publication is recycled and meets the minimum requirements of American National Standard for Information Sciences—Permanence of Paper for Printed Library Materials, ANSI Z39.48-1984.

101 DEVOTIONALS WITH CHILDREN
Copyright © 1999 by Herald Press, Scottdale, Pa. 15683
   Published simultaneously in Canada by Herald Press,
     Waterloo, Ont. N2L 6H7. All rights reserved
Library of Congress Catalog Card Number: 99-30151
International Standard Book Number: 0-8361-9117-X
Printed in the United States of America
Book design by Jim Butti

08 07 06 05 04 03 02 01 00 99 10 9 8 7 6 5 4 3 2 1

To order or request information, please call
1-800-759-4447 (individuals); 1-800-245-7894 (trade).
Website: www.mph.org

*To Joel, Melanie, and Perry*
*who gave me thumbs up on all 101 devotionals.*

*To Lauren, Preston, Adriane, Morgan, Laura, David,*
*Ben, Steve, Tony, Cheri, Kyle, Jessica, Austin, Jason,*
*Megan, Ingrid, and others who heard them.*

*To my friends who said, "You can do it," and to God,*
*for answering my prayers when I needed ideas.*

# Contents

# Words from the Author

## The Swing

How do you like to go up in a swing,
Up in the air so blue?
Oh, I do think it the pleasantest thing
Ever a child can do!

Up in the air and over the wall,
Till I can see so wide,
Rivers and trees and cattle and all
Over the countryside—

Till I look down on the garden green,
Down on the roof so brown
Up in the air I go flying again,
Up in the air and down!

**—Robert Louis Stevenson**

    I may have written my first devotional when my mother pushed me on the swing in our backyard. She came from the garden on the other side of the sweet-smelling Russian olive trees, wiped her hands on her apron, pulled the swing way back, so that I thought I might fall, and then let me fly.

    With each push, she said a line from Robert Louis Stevenson's poem. Its rhythm swayed back and forth. The poem matched everything I was feeling, except I could see that our roof was green, not brown. I wanted to rewrite the poem, but "green" didn't rhyme with "down."

    Swinging in the backyard, riding my stick horse,

walking out to fetch the cows, and picking strawberries were all devotional times for me as a child. They meant I was with my family. Whether we were laughing or crying, working or playing, eating or sleeping, we were being family together.

Mom taught me to see creation as God's handiwork. Dad taught me what it meant to live in community. Nelson carried me around like a sack of flour and held me when my cousin Janie died. Dorothy and I chased pigs together when they all got out. Edie listened to my questions about how God can hear everyone's prayers at once. My family was like a mini-world where I discovered a loving God who cared about me and about all people.

I invite you to take time to absorb the meaning of these devotionals. Spend time in prayer together, and share your stories. The devotionals are arranged in biblical order, but you can read them in any order. Change the names of the characters, if you like, so they have special meaning to your family and culture. Add your favorite songs to the devotional time. Allow yourself the freedom to come to God as you are and to take away from the time a new sense of God's presence with you.

—June Galle Krehbiel

# 1

## Read Genesis 1:1-5*

*And God said, "Let there be light,"*
*and there was light (Genesis 1:3).*

### Pancake Creations

Joel was making pancakes. Flour, sugar, baking powder, a cup of milk, two tablespoons of oil, a dash of salt. "You do the dash of salt," Joel told Mom. "I don't know how."

"Hold out your hand," Mom said. She sprinkled a few grains of salt into his palm.

"What good does that do?" Joel asked.

"A little salt helps food taste better," Mom said. Joel cupped his hand to sprinkle the salt into the mixing bowl.

Later he set a plate of hot pancakes onto the table. Joel said, "Let there be pancakes," and there were pancakes.

God made the world. But God didn't need a recipe. God didn't use any utensils or ingredients we think we need to make things. With a power we can't understand, God created the world and everything in it. God made the sun and other stars, all the planets and their moons. God, the one we call friend, is also God the Creator—*our* Creator.

Just as Joel combined all the ingredients to make tasty pancakes, God made each of us a perfect and wonderful human being.

What ingredients do you think God could have stirred together to create you?

***Scripture passages with asterisks are suitable for young readers.***

**Prayer:** Thank you, God, for all of your creation, and thank you, God, for making me. Amen.

**Clincher:**

> *(Clap hands seven times in rhythm.)*
> Clap your hands and stomp your feet;
> God's creation is a treat.
> *(Clap seven times.)*
> Clap your hands and touch the ground;
> God's creation is around.
> *(Clap seven times.)*
> *(Add your own lines of seven beats.)*

# 2

## Read Genesis 1:24-25

*In Joppa there was a disciple named Tabitha (which, when translated, is Dorcas), who was always doing good and helping the poor (Acts 9:36).*

### Gazelles

Next to the nearly dry riverbed, Sulemani spotted tracks. Gazelles had come, seeking water and leaving their tracks in the soft mud. Sulemani wished he had been there to see his favorite animals. He liked their soft eyes, their curvy horns, and, most of all, their speed. They had come at daybreak, and he had missed them.

Early the next morning, Sulemani returned to the riverbed to wait for the gazelles. He saw them approach, ears and eyes alert. They drank from the river and then bounded away.

Antelopes, including gazelles, roam many parts of our earth, chewing their cud and running gracefully at top speed. Their hollow horns come in different shapes—some are straight, others twist and curve into corkscrews. God made them all "according to their kinds" (Genesis 1:25).

In Acts 9 we read about a disciple named Dorcas, whose name meant "gazelle." The Bible compares other persons to gazelles because they were fast runners. If God had not created animals, our world would be a much different place. We need to live along **with** the animals, as God meant for us to do, instead of competing against them.

If you could choose to be named after an animal, what would be your name?

15

**Prayer:** Great God, help us to remember that all life comes from you. Thank you for the living creatures of all kinds and for their place in the world. Amen.

**Clincher:**
>Oh, give me a home where the buffalo roam,
>Where the deer and the antelope play,
>Where seldom is heard a discouraging word
>And the skies are not cloudy all day.
>*—Cowboy song, possibly written by Brewster Higley*

# 3
## Read Genesis 2:1-3

*By the seventh day God had finished the work he had been doing; so on the seventh day he rested from all his work (Genesis 2:2).*

### Rests

Think of your favorite hymn or chorus. Now try singing it all the way through, without stopping for a breath. Can you do it? Probably not.

A few instruments, like violin or guitar, can play without stopping for a long time. But when they do, we expect a break of some kind—a pause or a rest. The best music pauses sometimes before going on.

God knows that rests are important. After creating the heavens and earth, God rested. God might have paused a bit after each day's labor, but on the seventh day God *rested*.

Some of us have a hard time resting. We want to keep on working or playing, but rest is important. Our bodies need rest, and our minds need rest. When we get the right amount of sleep, we feel refreshed and ready to go again.

Sing your song again, but this time break at the end of each thought or musical phrase. Think about God as you sing, and make this devotional time a time of rest.

**Prayer:** God, we ask that you will bless our rest and make it holy. Amen.

**Clincher:** The best eraser in the world is a good night's sleep.
　　*—O. A. Battista*

# 4

## Read Genesis 9:8-16

*Whenever the rainbow appears in the clouds, I will see it and remember the everlasting covenant between God and all living creatures of every kind on the earth (Genesis 9:16).*

### Promises

The two girls huddle together, sharing secrets. They whisper and look around for others who might be eavesdropping. Then one of the voices gets louder. "Please, tell me. Please, *please*. I won't tell. I promise. Cross my heart."

On New Year's Day, many people make resolutions for the New Year. They promise that for the entire year they will behave differently. What kinds of promises or New Year's resolutions have you made?

God made a promise. In a way it was like a New Year's resolution. After sending the great flood, which destroyed all the people on the earth except Noah and his family, God promised to never again destroy the earth. This kind of promise is called a *covenant*.

What promise can you make to God today? Light a candle to remind you of your promise.

**Prayer:** In my heart, Lord Jesus, I promise to share your love with everyone. Amen.

### Clincher:

As long as earth endures,
As long as years are new,
A friend I'll be to Jesus.
I promise this so true.

# 5

# Read Genesis 12:1-5

*The Lord had said to Abram, "Leave your country, your people and your father's household and go to the land I will show you" (Genesis 12:1).*

## Shoelaces

Karley rushed to tie her shoes. It seemed like whenever she wanted to hurry, the laces knotted up. Karley was so excited she couldn't think of anything except Dad's new job. She figured she was even more excited than he was. *Dad's* shoelaces hadn't caused him any trouble. Finally, she ran to the door and called, "I got myself all knotted up! But I'm ready to go."

Think about changes that have happened to you or someone in your family. How did you feel because of these changes? How was your life different?

God told Abram and Sarai to leave the place where they had lived for many years. They trusted God to guide them, and God promised to give them many children and grandchildren. Because of God's promise and because Abram and Sarai obeyed God, they became the people God wanted them to be. But they had to change.

When you put on your shoes the next time, think about God talking to you. What might God want you to change?

**Prayer:** Dear God, each day I take steps to follow you. Guide me as I try to be like you. Amen.

**Clincher:**
Everything changes but change.
*—Thomas Hardy*

19

# 6

## Read Genesis 13:1-2, 5-9

*Lot looked up and saw that the whole plain of the Jordan was well watered. . . . So Lot chose for himself the whole plain of the Jordan (Genesis 13:10-11).*

### Candy

For a long time Carlos stood in front of the counter, peering through the shiny glass to see the rows of candy for sale. The chocolates appealed to him the most; he could almost taste the malted milk balls, melting in his mouth until only the crunchy center remained. But the red licorice would be good too. He wondered how he would ever decide.

Which candy would you choose? How do *you* decide?

Some decisions are easy to make; others are harder. Abram and Lot had to make a decision about space. They realized that both of their families and all their animals could not live together. After Abram suggested going different ways and offered Lot first choice of the land, Lot had to make a decision. Abram made a good plan to help the families get along better. They agreed to separate so the fighting would stop.

Today when you make a decision, think of it as just one little candy in the dish of life. And be joyful!

**Prayer:** Dear God, please guide me in the decisions I make today. Amen.

**Clincher:**
Making up your mind is like making a bed; it usually helps to have someone on the other side.
   *—Gerald Horton Bath*

# 7

# Read Genesis 21:17-20*

*God was with the boy as he grew up*
*(Genesis 21:20a).*

## Hospital

Ryan lay in the hospital bed, a tube in his hand connecting him to the medicine that would make his fever come down from 104 degrees. For hours he lay there, watching drips of medicine ooze into his body. His mother sat beside him. Nurses floated in and out of the room. Ryan's mouth was so dry he felt like he'd been in the Sahara Desert all day.

"Want a sip of water?" Mom asked. Ryan wanted more than a sip. A whole swimming pool would be perfect, but he drank what she offered him. Sip by sip. Drip by drip. Slowly Ryan's temperature came down. By the next morning, he was playing a game of cards with Mom.

"I felt like I was drying up in the desert," he said. "What if you and the nurses hadn't been here to take care of me?"

"God was with you, too," Mom said. "God is always with you."

Family members, friends, neighbors, nurses, and doctors are often there to take care of us. But God is the best caregiver of all. Just as God took care of Ishmael and his mother, Hagar, God takes care of each of us.

Imagine God as the most caring nurse ever. Think about times in your life when God has cared for you. How did God give you what you needed or give people you know what they needed?

**Prayer:** Dear God, thank you for taking care of us all the time. Be with those who need your special care today. Help us to care for others as you have cared for us. Amen.

**Clincher:**
All night, all day,
Angels watchin' over me, my Lord;
All night, all day,
Angels watchin' over me.
*—Spiritual*

# 8

# Read Genesis 27:41-45; 33:1-4

*Lord, how many times shall I forgive my
brother? (Matthew 18:21).*

## Broken Windshield

Slivers of glass covered the floor of the car and
the front seat. Jon and his family stared at the
windshield, looking at the damage. Something powerful had hit the glass on the driver's side so hard
that it made a deep dent, causing the break to ripple
outward.

"Do you have any enemies?" the policeman asked
Jon's mother.

"Not that I can think of. I can't believe anyone did
this on purpose."

Jon thought Mom was wrong. Someone *had* done
it on purpose, and he was mad at whoever broke
their car's windshield.

For over a week, Jon was mad. He felt awful. His
anger changed how he felt about everything.

"I think what you need is a new window to your
heart," Mom told him.

"How do I get that?"

"By forgiving," she said.

Finally, after asking God to forgive whoever broke
their windshield, Jon felt like he had a new, clean,
unshattered window to his heart. He wasn't mad at
the person anymore, and he wasn't mad at himself
for feeling angry.

Jesus tells us to forgive—not just seven times, as
Peter suggested, but seventy-seven times. Jesus must
have known how easy it is to be angry and to hold
those angry feelings inside of us for a long time.

Forgiveness lets us get rid of the anger and think about relationships again.

**Prayer:** Come into my heart, loving God, and help me forgive. Amen.

**Clincher:**
> To err is human, to forgive, divine.
> *—Alexander Pope*

# 9

# Read Genesis 28:10-16

*The Lord will watch over your coming and going both now and forevermore (Psalm 121:8).*

## Old Shep

Old Shep smelled the rabbit. His eyes were almost blind, and his legs were weak from arthritis, but Shep's nose still wrinkled at the scent of a rabbit hopping across the field. "Woof! Woof! Woof!"

"What do you want, Shep?" Irvin yelled, as he walked from the house. "You want me to catch the rabbit for you?"

"Woof! Woof! Woof!" old Shep barked.

It's amazing how animals sometimes seem to talk to us. God communicates with us in amazing ways, too. God talked to Jacob in a dream, and Jacob realized it was God leading him. "God was here," he said.

Has God talked to you—through a dream, through music, art, or nature? Did you feel God's presence—during a friend's visit, in quiet worship time, or when you were sick? God's time with you may be dramatic or calm, loud or quiet. And, no matter whether we've just biked ten miles or been wakened from a night's sleep on a rock, God can speak and we can listen.

What is *your* favorite way to communicate with God?

**Prayer:** Dear God, just as you talked to Jacob at Bethel, lead me in an everlasting visit with you. Amen.

**Clincher:** It's me, it's me, it's me, oh, Lord, standin' in the need of prayer.
    —*Spiritual*

25

# 10

# Read Exodus 2:1-10

*But when [Moses' mother] could hide him no longer, she got a papyrus basket for him and coated it with tar and pitch. Then she placed the child in it and put it among the reeds along the bank of the Nile (Exodus 2:3).*

### Hide and Seek

Kyle squatted behind the bushy spirea shrubs, trying to hide during the Sunday afternoon game of hide-and-seek. ***What's taking them so long?*** he wondered. ***Did they forget me?***

Just then his big brother Jimmy crawled in beside him. "They're still looking for us. Be real quiet," Jimmy whispered. For a long time they waited. They watched as black shoes stepped around the bushes and climbed the porch steps. Then their aunt's searching eyes met theirs. "Here they are!" she yelled. "You boys were harder to find than Moses in the bulrushes!"

Just as Moses' family cared for him, healthy families today take care of each other. With Sunday afternoon games and bedtime hugs, families surround each other with love and care. God put us in families so we can love and care for each other. We are families. We are good. And good is only one letter away from "God."

**Prayer:** Dear God and Maker of families, thank you for your love and care. Thank you for our families. Amen.

### Clincher:

A mother is not a person to lean on, but a person to make leaning unnecessary.
    —*Dorothy Canfield Fisher*

# 11

## Read Exodus 3:13-15

*This is my name forever, the name by which
I am to be remembered from generation to generation
(Exodus 3:15).*

### Fig Newtons

On the small, low shelf, just inside the door to Grandma's kitchen, sat the brown ceramic cookie jar. Often when Anna and her cousins visited their grandparents, they found the cookie jar filled with store-bought Fig Newtons. The cousins didn't like these flat cookies filled with sticky figs, but Anna loved them. The only time she ever got to eat them was at her grandparents' house.

Once, on the way home from the store, when Anna had squeezed a Fig Newtons package too tight, filling squeezed out of some of the cookies. "That's the way it is with a grandparent's love," Grandma told Anna. "Squeeze too tight and grandchildren will just pop out of grandma's hugs. I learned that from *my* grandma."

What family traditions do you continue in *your* home? Many good family traditions keep going for years. One of those is a love for God. Another is a love for each other. From parents to children, from grandparents to grandchildren, love stays the same. We might show it in different ways, but it is still the same.

How do you know that your family loves you? How do you know God loves you?

**Prayer:** May the God of all generations hug us with a love of gentleness and compassion, forever and ever. Amen.

27

**Clincher:**

My grandma's hugs smell like tomatoes and turnips that she says are good for me to eat.

My grandma's hugs taste like sour cream cookies that she made for me and Grandpa.

My grandma's hugs sound like a tune she hums when she's rocking my baby cousin.

I wonder what God's hugs are like.

# 12

## Read Exodus 16:11-16

*When the dew was gone, thin flakes like frost on the
ground appeared on the desert floor. When the Israelites
saw it, they said to each other, "What is it?"
(Exodus 16:14-15a).*

### Grape

In the restaurant, Simon popped a grape into his
mouth. "What is it?" he said, when this grape tasted
salty instead of sweet. Puzzled, he glanced at the
other people at his table. His big sister sat across from
him, a funny smile on her face. "Do you like the
olive?" she asked. She knew Simon had never eaten
black olives before.

In the desert, the Hebrews ate a food they had
never eaten before. It was a special food God provided for them during their escape from Egypt. The
beginning of the word *manna*, "man," is a question
in the Hebrew language. The second part of the
word, "hu," makes the Hebrew question, "What is
it?" The Hebrew people wanted to know what they
were eating.

Although people who study the Bible are not
exactly sure what manna was, Exodus 16:31 says it
was white and tasted like wafers made with honey.
To the Hebrews, manna meant life. It was food from
God.

Today God provides for our needs, too. All good
things come from God. When you need a time of
rest, someone to listen to you and guide you, God
will be there.

**Prayer:** You are with us, God the Provider, all

29

through our lives. Thank you for your presence within us. Amen.

**Clincher:** What kind of ice cream dessert did Moses serve the Israelites when they left Egypt? *Manna-splits!*

# 13

## Read Exodus 20:1-3*

*We know that the law is good
if one uses it properly (1 Timothy 1:8).*

**Most Unusual Law**

Once upon a time, a most unusual ruler in a most unusual city called all the people together and read a proclamation:

I order that all red traffic lights mean GO
and that all green traffic lights mean STOP.
This order begins immediately.

When the people heard this, they said, "That's a most unusual law." They were used to going when they saw a green light and stopping for a red one. But they set out to follow the new order.

Visitors to the city and travelers on the main highway, though, knew nothing about The Most Unusual Law. When visiting drivers drove through green traffic lights and local people drove through red ones, things got all mixed up.

The same thing happens in our lives when we don't follow the rules God set up for us. The Ten Commandments, given to the Hebrew people more than 3,300 years ago, are just as important for people today as they were then. God's rules are not confusing. They make sense.

**Prayer:** Dear God, thank you for the rules you have given us for living. Amen.

**Clincher:**

The next time you see a green traffic light,
Ask yourself simply, "Am I doing all right?
Am I driving ahead in God's perfect plan?
Am I turning to Jesus whenever I can?"

# 14

## Read Numbers 6:24-26*

*May God be gracious to us and bless us
and make his face shine upon us (Psalm 67:1).*

**Good-bye**

Shayla leaned against the car and tried to hold
back the tears. How could she ever say good-bye to
her only sister? Why did her sister want to go work
in another country, anyway? Why did she have to
leave for two years? Shayla heard her sister say good-
bye to their grandmother. Grandmother said, "God
be with you. Go in peace." Encouraged by
Grandmother's words, Shayla hugged her sister
through the car window. They said good-bye, and
the car drove away.

Can you think of times when someone close to
you went away for a long time? What do you remember about it?

The word "good-bye" is short for the words, *God
be with you.* We say the word often, showing that
God's presence makes it easier when someone goes
away. Whether separations last for two weeks or two
years, they are a natural part of life. So God has given
us words of blessing, like those found in Numbers 6.
Use these words as your prayer today.

**Prayer:**

The Lord bless you and keep you;
the Lord make his face shine upon you
and be gracious to you;
the Lord turn his face toward you
and give you peace. Amen.

**Clincher:**

Adios. Espero verte de nuevo lo que será un verdadero placer el hacerlo.

(A farewell from the Dominican Republic, spoken in Spanish, translated, "Good-bye. I hope to see you again. It will be a pleasure for me to see you again.")

*—from Ulises Garcia*

# 15

# Read Deuteronomy 6:5-9

*Love the Lord your God with all your heart
and with all your soul and with all your strength
(Deuteronomy 6:5).*

## Squirrel

In early spring, high up in the oak tree, a brown squirrel clung to the tip of a thin branch. A breeze tossed the tree, but the squirrel held on. With its front feet, it grabbed at new leaves that were pushing from the branches. Stuffing the leaves into its mouth, the squirrel ate as if it had been hungry all winter. For almost an hour, it moved from branch to branch, devouring the tastiest young leaves.

When we have the chance, we enjoy our favorite foods. Sometimes we stuff them down, like a squirrel chomping on young leaves. Sometimes we carefully taste each bit, until it slides slowly down. A favorite song, book, or hobby can interest us so much that we forget the time. Hours pass, as we give full attention to one of our favorite pastimes.

God expects that kind of attention, too. We are to love our God with heart, soul, and strength. Imagine a world where all people everywhere devote all their energy to loving God. Imagine a world where all people love God with the same strength that God loves us!

**Prayer:** Dear God, may our lives burst with your love today. Amen.

**Clincher:** If you could spend a whole day on your favorite pastime, what would you do?

35

# 16

## Read Joshua 24:23-24*

*"Now then," said Joshua, "throw away the foreign gods that are among you and yield your hearts to the Lord, the God of Israel" (Joshua 24:23).*

### Rototiller

BRRRRRRRR. The roar of the rototiller destroyed the quiet in Mary's private hideaway. Gone were the wren's warble and the cardinal's chirp. Gone were the two new kittens, scared away by the noise. It was even hard for Mary to read. The harsh noise seemed to drill into her brain. Then, as suddenly as it started, the rototiller stopped. Mary could hear the birds again. Soon the kittens were back, swatting at her shoestrings. It was easy to read. Mary felt part of the life around her again.

Sometimes things that happen in our lives keep us from being close to God. We feel cut off from the beautiful parts of life. We no longer hear the sounds of nature, or enjoy our friends or pets. When that happens, we need a Joshua to tell us to ignore the things that harm our relationship with God. And we can promise to serve and obey God, perhaps in a way we have never done before.

**Prayer:** Dear God, like the Israelites of long ago, I choose to serve and obey you. I dedicate this day to you. Amen.

### Clincher:

Whoever desires to be a new being but cannot leave behind the old life is like a pig that has just been washed and returns promptly to the mud puddle.
    —*Hans Denck, 1526, German Anabaptist*

# 17

## Read 1 Samuel 3:1-10

*Then the Lord called Samuel.*
*Samuel answered, "Here I am" (1 Samuel 3:4).*

### Storm

Heavy rain pounded on the roof. Lightning broke the darkness. Thunder stomped from one side of the apartment to the other. Ian, lying in bed, felt his heart racing. The hall light went on, and he saw his dad's face. "Just checking the windows," Dad said. "That last thunderclap was a big one. You know, my grand-dad used to tell me that thunder was God walking across the sky. Try to go back to sleep now. Good night."

Ian thought about God. He knew thunder happened because of a giant electrical charge, but knowing God was there in the thunder made him feel better.

God talks to us in many ways. We wish God would walk into our home and start talking, but that doesn't usually happen. Samuel got a call at nighttime. He thought it was Eli, but it was the voice of God. Without Eli's help to understand what was happening, Samuel might have missed hearing God. Ian's dad helped him to hear God in the storm. Many times God speaks to us through other persons who guide us or help us. When have you felt God's presence?

**Prayer:** Dear God, we pray in the dark of night and in the light of day. We want to talk with you, to hear your call, and to respond. Amen.

### Clincher:

When I pray
an enormous ear strains to hear me.
    —*Yorifumi Yaguchi*

# 18

## Read 1 Samuel 16:1, 10-13

*So Samuel asked Jesse, "Are these all the sons you have?" "There is still the youngest," Jesse answered, "but he is tending the sheep" (1 Samuel 16:11a).*

### Youngest

Skip felt left out again. "Someday you'll be old enough to go to a party with your friends," Skip's sister told him before she left. His older sisters and brothers did lots of things he couldn't. He had to go to bed earlier than anyone else. He had the smallest closet. No one ever asked him for *his* advice. And he always ended up having to do the worst jobs.

David, the harp-playing shepherd boy, was the youngest son, too. But one day someone called David from his job of herding sheep. Probably still smelling like the sheep, David walked into his father's tent, and Jesse chose him to be anointed for service to God. From the smallest clan, of the smallest tribe, Jesse's youngest son was chosen by God to become king over all Israel.

People of all ages, abilities, sizes, and appearances can serve God. How will you serve God today?

**Prayer:** God of all people, I come to you as I am. Please accept me for your service today. Amen.

**Clincher:** Using drops of baby oil or hand lotion, anoint each other for God's service by rubbing it on each other's hands. Say: "We are your servants, O God."

# 19

# Read 1 Samuel 20:42*

*A friend loves at all times  (Proverbs 17:17).*

### In the Doghouse

Sox and Taffy were best friends. They slept together in the doghouse, ate dog food out of the same dish, licked each other's faces, and played tag with each other. Sox was a cat, and Taffy was a dog, but Taffy never chased Sox, and Sox was never afraid of Taffy. They each needed a companion, so they became friends, even though cats and dogs are often enemies.

Sometimes people treat each other like enemies, bickering and fighting over things that don't seem important. Even at those times, friendships can develop that are stronger than any hate. David, the one anointed by Samuel to be king of Israel, became friends with Jonathan, the son of jealous King Saul, who hated David.

Imagine a life without any friends. Can you name every one of your friends? As you pray, spend time in silence, thanking God for your friends. May you be as good a friend to others as God is to you.

**Prayer:** Dear God and Friend to all, thank you for friends. Amen.

**Clincher:**
Three things are important in this world:
Good health,
Peace with one's neighbor,
Friendship with all.
—*Traditional saying from the Serer people,*
*West Africa*

# 20

# Read 1 Kings 3:5-9

*Happy are those who find wisdom, and those who get understanding (Proverbs 3:13, NRSV).*

## Mice

Once upon a time, behind a set of encyclopedias, there lived a family of mice. One day, the biggest mouse said, "We need to be smarter. If we eat all of these books, I know we will be filled with knowledge." Inspired by this new wisdom, the mice began eating. By the end of the month, they had chewed through all the books. They felt fuller than they had ever felt in their lives, but they did not feel smarter. A visiting cat happened by and laughed.

"You might be full of knowledge," the cat said, "but you certainly aren't very wise."

Solomon, the young king, asked God for an understanding heart, so he could lead God's people well. Even the wisest people realize they don't know everything. Most of us won't ever be as wise as Solomon or be able to govern and write like he did, but all of us have some wisdom. We can make wise choices and deal with people in wise ways. We recognize what is right and what is wrong. And the wisest among us are probably those who are able to love all people.

**Prayer:** Almighty God, you are wiser than Solomon. Give me, your servant, an understanding heart, to know the difference between right and wrong. Amen.

**Clincher:** When God says, "Ask," what will I say that *I* want?

# 21

# Read 1 Kings 5:1, 12, 18

*When Hiram king of Tyre heard that Solomon had been anointed king to succeed his father David, he sent his envoys to Solomon . . .  There were peaceful relations between Hiram and Solomon . . . (1 Kings 5:1a, 12a).*

## More Dessert

"Hey, Mom, can you get me some more dessert?" Jeremiah asked. Mom stopped eating and looked him straight in the eye. A hint of a smile showed on her face.

"Are your legs broken?" she asked. Jeremiah's legs were *not* broken. He'd heard this question from Mom other times, and he knew her next line, too. "If you want life to happen, you have to take the first step."

Peace happens the same way. People who believe peace is important practice peace every day. They know the first step is reaching out to family, neighbors, and strangers. Peace is an action, not just a thought.

When Hiram, king of Tyre, heard that Solomon had become king, he took the first step in making peace between the two nations. He sent a group of people to be friends with Solomon. Because of that first step of peace, Solomon provided food for Hiram's household in exchange for building materials for the temple.

Think about what you might do to take a step toward peace this day.

**Prayer:** Dear God, help me to step into shoes fit for acts of peace. Amen.

**Clincher:**
I can make peace with everyone I meet . . .
Make peace and it can't be beat.
It's something I can do and it's real important too.
I can make peace, it's true.
*—Jude and Doug Krehbiel*

# 22

## Read 2 Kings 4:8-11*

*One day Elisha went to Shunem. And a well-to-do woman was there, who urged him to stay for a meal. So whenever he came by, he stopped there to eat (2 Kings 4:8).*

### Overnight Guests

*Knock. Knock. Knock.* The door opens. "Come in. Come in," the hostess says, her voice raised in excitement. "I'm so glad you decided to stay with us. Here, let me take your coats. I was worried about you. I was afraid you got lost. You must be tired. Let me show you where you'll sleep. Then we'll eat something."

In any part of the world, a comfortable bed and a tasty meal are welcome to a tired traveler. Like the family in Shunem, who welcomed Elisha, many Christians serve God by taking in guests. We call this *hospitality,* which comes from a Latin word meaning "guest" or "visitor." There are different ways to show hospitality in different places. In villages in India, any visitor is expected to drink a cup of hot tea. The visitor stays at least as long as it takes to prepare the tea, serve it, and drink it—enough time for the guest and the host to talk.

What does hospitality mean where you live?

**Prayer:** Dear God, make us willing servants as we give hospitality to others. Amen.

**Clincher:**
Let me live in a house by the side of the road
and be a friend to man.
    —*Sam Walter Foss*

43

# 23

## Read Nehemiah 1:5-6

*O Lord, God of heaven, the great and awesome God,
who keeps his covenant of love with those who love
him and obey his commands (Nehemiah 1:5).*

### Peanut Butter Cup

Christina handed the clerk the money and picked
up her candy bar. "Why did you get one of those?"
her friend Rhonda asked. "I thought you didn't like
that kind."

Christina looked at the candy in the bright orange
wrapper. "I never tried it before. I guess I just *thought*
I wouldn't like it." She pulled open the wrapper and
licked the chocolate coating.

"You've gotta *bite* it," said Rhonda. "The best
part's in the middle."

Slowly, Christina bit into the soft center.
Chocolate and peanut butter flavors blended together.
"It's wonderful!" she yelled.

Some of us treat God the same way. We keep God
at a distance and don't try very hard to find out who
God is. We say words of prayers without feeling the
relationship God will give us, if we just sink our teeth
in. The best experiences in prayer happen when we
put our whole selves into it. Only then can we celebrate our relationship with God.

**Prayer:** Dear God, guide us into a loving relationship with you. We pray this in your name. Amen.

**Clincher:** Praying to God is like sinking your teeth
into a chocolate peanut butter cup.

# 24

# Read Psalm 8

*When I consider your heavens, the work of your fingers, the moon and the stars, which you have set in place, what is man that you are mindful of him? (Psalm 8:3-4a).*

**Rug**

Jennifer fingered the rug, woven in shades of pink and lavender on a royal blue background. "It looks like a sunset, Mrs. DeLay. Where are you going to hang it?" Jennifer asked.

"Oh, it's not for me. I made it for the hospital benefit auction."

"But it's so pretty, and you spent so much time on it. How can you give it away?"

"I'll get more pleasure from giving it away than keeping it for myself," Mrs. DeLay said. "That way others can enjoy it too."

We humans often look at God's heavenly creation the same way Jennifer looked at the beautiful rug. Creation is woven together in colors and patterns as rich and varied as the nature of God. David describes the heavens as the work of God's fingers. Each detail of God's creation teaches us about God's majesty.

What part of nature do you find the most amazing?

**Prayer:** O Lord, how majestic you are! Thank you for the beautiful creation that you put in place for us to share with you. Amen.

**Clincher:**
Love all God's creation,
both the whole and every grain of sand.

Love every leaf, every ray of light.
Love the animals, love the plants,
love each separate thing.
If you love each thing,
you will perceive
the mystery of God in all.
   —*Fyodor Mikhaylovich Dostoyevsky*

# 25

## Read Psalm 23

*I will fear no evil, for you are with me; your rod and your staff, they comfort me (Psalm 23:4b).*

### Stuck in the Mud

After a summer downpour, Andrew plodded through the mud to finish his chores, in boots that were much too large. Each step felt heavy as he strained to pull his boots out of the mud. Mud sloshed on his bare legs and ran into his boots. Then he stepped into deeper mud and got stuck. Andrew pulled and tugged, but the boots held fast. He undid the clasps and slipped his feet out of the boots. With bare feet, Andrew ran through the mud until he reached lush, green grass.

Sometimes things that happen in our lives make us feel as heavy and tired as walking in deep mud with big boots. We plod along, feeling like we might be stuck in this bad situation forever. We are lonely, sad, afraid, or worried, and things seem hopeless.

In Psalm 23, David wrote about the care and comfort God gave him. We can step out of bad situations, too, and run barefoot to God, who gives us the care we need.

**Prayer:** Dear God, step into the hearts of all of us who are hurting, and bring us your peace. Amen.

**Clincher:**
Without a shepherd, sheep are not a flock.
*—Russian proverb*

# 26

## Read Psalm 30:4-5*

*Sing to the Lord, you saints of his; praise his holy name. For his anger lasts only a moment, but his favor lasts a lifetime (Psalm 30:4-5a).*

### Appaloosa

Lynn searched the rows of shelves in the large department store for the perfect gift for her friend. There were magazines, candy, towels, glasses, T-shirts, watches, purses, jewelry, socks, perfumes, and furniture. Lynn wanted to give something that would last a long time. Then she spotted a beautiful figurine of an Appaloosa horse, its head tilted upward, as if begging Lynn to buy it. She knew her friend could keep the gift for many years.

Some things, like sandcastles, last a short time. Others last a long time. God's favor lasts forever. Some people go through life believing God is angry with them for something they did. They have a hard time believing God could ever love them.

If we think God is angry with us all the time, then we are angry with God and with other people. If we believe God approves of us, then we approve of God and others. Psalm 30, verse 5, promises us that God's anger lasts for only a moment, but God's favor lasts a lifetime.

**Prayer:** Dear God, with thanksgiving and honor we come to you. Show us your loving favor. Amen.

**Clincher:**
Never answer a letter while you are angry.
—*Chinese proverb*

# 27
## Read Psalm 33:1-3

*Sing to [the Lord] a new song; . . . shout for joy*
*(Psalm 33:3).*

### Shout

Imagine you're at a ballgame. The score is tied, with only seconds to go. The home team is close to scoring, but the fans and the players on the bench sit calmly. They look like they're enjoying a music concert. They watch their team score, clap politely, and go home.

Sound realistic? No way! Few tie ballgames end with fans and players sitting calmly. Sometimes the roar of the crowd is deafening. Exciting games make excited fans.

God's fans shout, too. We shout when we feel God working in our lives. We shout when God's choices are our choices. We shout when we feel God's creative touch in the world. We shout when peace happens. We shout when we love all people, including ourselves. We shout because God told us to *shout for joy*.

When did you shout for joy? What times *should* we shout for joy?

**Prayer:** Because we are your fans, great God, WE SHOUT FOR JOY. Amen.

### Clincher:

Shout <u>first</u> for our <u>God</u> who <u>always</u> knows the <u>score;</u>
Shout <u>next</u> for our <u>God</u> who <u>hears</u> us when we <u>snore;</u>
Shout <u>now</u> for our <u>God</u> who's <u>not</u> a dino<u>saur;</u>
Shout <u>last</u> for our <u>God</u> who <u>loves</u> us more and <u>more.</u>

49

# 28

## Read Psalm 51:7*

*Wash me, and I will be whiter than snow
(Psalm 51:7b).*

### Sugar, Milk, Snow

Sugar, milk, snow. How are these three alike? *(Pause for response.)* If you said they are all white, you're right.

Because white reflects light, it's so bright it can hurt our eyes. In winter, when snow covers everything outside, sunshine makes the snow dazzling bright. The earth seems completely new. Nothing looks the same.

The same surprise happens when we wash a dirty shirt with soap. Colors dulled by dirt become bright. In fact, anything we wash—clothes, hands, hair, windows, yes, even the family dog—can look new.

The writer of this Bible verse wants to be a new person. He asks God for a washing that will make him more dazzling than snow. Imagine God holding you above a large basin of water, gently dunking and scrubbing you in bubbly soap until you are sparkling clean. Of course, no one can be scrubbed whiter than snow, but God can make us new on the inside—if we ask.

**Prayer:** Dear God, wash away the parts of our lives that are dirty, and make us new. Amen.

**Clincher:**

> Wash me clean in my heart, in my heart, in my
> heart,
> Wash me clean in my heart today.
> Wash me clean in my heart, in my heart, in my
> heart,
> Wash me clean in my heart, I pray.

# 29

## Read Psalm 96

*Worship the Lord in the splendor of*
*his holiness; tremble before him, all the earth*
*(Psalm 96:9).*

### Ocean

Shelly sat on a rocky cliff overlooking the ocean. Below, endless waves rolled in, crashing against the rocks and spraying her with water. Far away she could see a ship. Seagulls dove for fish, scooping them out of the water. Above, the sky arched in a grand display of cloud ribbons floating against a clear, blue background. "If God is greater than all this, everyone on earth should worship God," Shelly said.

The writer of this psalm calls God "great" and "worthy of praise." If we believe God is more powerful, more majestic, and more awesome than any being that will ever live, then we, too, must worship the Lord. What a great God! What a great God!

List words that describe God's majesty.

**Prayer:** Great God, ruler of the sky and sea, I bow to worship you. I give you praise. You are the one God in my life. Amen.

### Clincher:

God is
Bigger than all the buildings in the world.
More majestic than all the rulers on earth.
More loving than all love everywhere.
Greater than the skies and all the seas.
Wiser than all the wisdom humans will ever know.
God is a great God.

# 30

## Read Psalm 100*

*Worship the Lord with gladness; come before him with joyful songs (Psalm 100:2).*

**Cars**

Less than a minute after Robbie got home, he had changed his clothes, put on his old cap, and headed out to the shed. There, in the corner, sat his old car, surrounded by greasy tools. Robbie got to work, unscrewing bolts to remove the old battery. He hummed a happy tune. He loved working on old cars.

How do you like to spend your free time?

Like Robbie, we all like to spend our free time on favorite activities. They give us a lot of happiness, whether we're skating, singing, sewing, or sailing.

In the same way we enjoy our times of play, we can enjoy our times of worship. Psalm 100 calls us to praise and worship the Lord with gladness. No matter where we are, we are to be happy when we worship God, singing songs of praise to the One who made us. We can be just as excited about worship as we are about our hobbies.

What are ways you can honor God and be happy in worship?

**Prayer:** Dear God, we worship you, with a burst of energy that brings praise and honor to your name. Amen.

**Clincher:**

In worship, as in no other way, we the church become the living body of Christ.

—*Eleanor Graber Kreider*

# 31

## Read Psalm 102:25-27

*But you remain the same, and your years*
*will never end (Psalm 102:27).*

**Rags**

The kitchen drawer was full of old clothes and linens. They made good rags for cleaning windows and wiping up spills. Kevin searched through the drawer, looking for a large rag. "What's this?" he asked his mom. It was a faded, torn piece of cloth, larger than the others.

"That used to be a tablecloth," Mom said. "It came from my great uncle's place. I used it for a few years, until it wore through. It's probably 40 or 50 years old."

"Can I use it on my bike?"

"Sure."

Look around you. What has changed where you live? Change is normal. We grow and mature. Accidents happen, and people die. Over time, even rocks and concrete change. Is there anything that doesn't change?

Psalm 102 tells us God stays the same. God is God, now and forever. We are like clothing that changes with time, but God is like a garment that never wears out.

**Prayer:** We praise you, God, because you are forever and ever and ever. Amen.

**Clincher:**

Jesus, Rock of ages, let me hide myself in thee.
Jesus, living Water, let me drink from your flowing
    stream.
—*M. Gerald Derstine*

# 32

## Read Psalm 119:102-105

*Your word is a lamp to my feet and a light for my path (Psalm 119:105).*

### Shadow Tag

It was late evening. The streetlight was shining brightly enough to play shadow tag. Near the light, the players' shadows were clear and dark. Far away, the shadows were hard to see. Jan was "it." She had caught almost all the other players by stepping on their shadows. Suddenly the streetlight went out. The game wasn't fun anymore, so everyone headed for the house—and light.

We use many kinds of light to brighten the hours after dark. Electric lights, flashlights, lanterns, and candles give us light for different activities. Without any kind of light, we are in the dark. Sometimes we use those same words, "in the dark," to describe not being able to understand something.

People in Bible times didn't have large streetlights. They used lamps, torches, and candles for lighting the path. Even a small light can show the way. That's the way it is with the verses in the Bible. In Psalm 119, one verse compares God's word to a lamp that lights the path for one's feet. Using God's Word, the Bible, we can find the way God wants us to go, and we can see what lies ahead for us.

What Bible verses have guided you? Which ones are your favorites?

**Prayer:** Dear God, help us to understand your word, and lighten our way. Amen.

54

**Clincher:**
> The word of God will guide my feet
>   wherever I may go.
> The word of God will teach to me
>   the things I ought to know.
> —*Traditional*

# 33

## Read Psalm 122:1*

*I rejoiced with those who said to me, "Let us go to the house of the Lord" (Psalm 122:1).*

### Four Minutes Past Midnight

At exactly four minutes past midnight, Kreg woke up. For a long time he lay in bed, thinking about the next day. He couldn't remember ever feeling this excited before. He heard Grandma walk past his door as she finished last-minute preparations. *She's as excited as I am,* he thought. Grandma had laughed so loud after he arrived that he knew she was eager for the holiday to start.

For Kreg, happiness meant a special holiday. For Grandma, it probably meant having Kreg with her. Happiness comes in different ways to different people. Some enjoy mastering new skills—like finally learning how to skate, play an instrument, or do handstands. Some get happiness from training a pet, watching a sunset, or making a friend laugh. Think about what makes you happy.

We feel happy deep inside when we worship God. Like the writer of Psalm 122, who rejoiced in worship, we can feel God's presence at any time, alone with God or in a group with God. Christians everywhere like to worship with other Christians.

As you worship God now, sing your favorite song that helps you worship, and pray with joy in your heart.

**Prayer:** We worship you with happiness, Lord of lords. May we worship you with hearts and minds and souls forever. Amen.

56

**Clincher:**
Joyfully, joyfully serving the King,
Joyfully, joyfully praises we sing,
Loyally, loyally striving to do
Something for Jesus
the whole journey through.
—*Lizzie De Armond*

# 34

## Read Psalm 133

*How very good and pleasant it is when kindred live together in unity! (Psalm 133:1, NRSV).*

### Mountain Dew

Glistening dew covered each blade of grass in the mountain meadow. Stepping out of her tent, Amy marveled at the way the dew sparkled in the sun. Wild strawberries blossomed near the stream that tumbled its way down the mountain. Squirrels scampered up the tall, straight lodgepole pines that sprouted from the mountainside. The early morning sun peeked over a ridge, and Amy heard laughter from a nearby tent. "Thank you, God," she prayed.

Psalm 133 says that living together in unity is as refreshing to our spirits as early morning dew on the mountain. Dew that forms during the night is a welcome drink for plants in dry climates. Bible passages use the word *dew* as a symbol of blessing or refreshment.

When we live, work, and play with others, we can choose how we relate to them. We can choose togetherness or we can choose apart-ness. We can choose to spend our time as individuals or as a community. Whether we think about it or not, we do affect the people, plants, and animals around us. We can choose to be like fire that destroys life or like dew that refreshes.

**Prayer:** Gentle Spirit of God, touch our souls with your refreshing spirit, and let us live in harmony with all beings. Amen.

**Clincher:** Unity: Just Dew It!

# **35**

## Read Psalm 139:14*

*I praise you, for I am fearfully and wonderfully made.
Wonderful are your works; that I know very well
(Psalm 139:14, NRSV).*

### Machine

Randy was fascinated during his tour through a factory. He watched big machines cut and form long sheets of steel into parts for other machines. The tour guide described each step and explained how accurate the large roll-forming machine could be in cutting the steel. "Within .001 of a inch," she said.

Randy's eyes opened wide. He couldn't imagine a machine so exact! How could a human being design it? "Only one thing works with more accuracy than this machine," the guide said. "Your body."

Randy laughed when he compared his own body to the huge machine beside him. The machine was large and noisy. It needed someone to run it. ***Bet it can't run downstairs every morning for breakfast,*** he thought.

No machine can compare with the human body. We are "fearfully and wonderfully made." Scientists, doctors, and nurses understand many details about how the human body works, but there are still many mysteries only God knows. Let us praise and honor our God, the Creator.

**Prayer:** Creator and wise God, for each part of my body, I praise you and thank you. Amen.

**Clincher:**

59

# 36

## Read Psalm 148

*Praise the Lord. Praise the Lord from the heavens, praise him in the heights above (Psalm 148:1).*

### Quasars

"Wow!" Tyler said, jumping down from his bunk bed. "Listen to this, Mark. There's something out there that's so big, its light takes ten billion years to reach us."

"What is it?" asked Mark. He had seldom seen his big brother so excited.

"It's called a *quasar*," Tyler said, skimming down the page of his book.

"Is it headed this way?" Mark asked.

"Mark, even if it is, we don't have to worry about it. It's too far away. Actually, there are more than five thousand quasars. They're made up of gases, and they're really bright and hot, and somebody discovered them in 1963, and . . ."

Mark interrupted. "I bet God knew they were there all along."

Tyler stared at his little brother. "I bet you're right. Yeah, I bet you're right."

Just when we humans think we've finally begun to understand everything God has created, we discover another part of life we didn't know about before. The amazing thing about creation is that God made everything. It is God we praise in Psalm 148.

Angels, heavens, sun, moon, and stars are included in the same psalm of praise with animals, birds, and people. God made them all, including quasars the size of our solar system, and kids the size of Mark and Tyler. Some parts of God's creation we can understand much better than other parts, but all of the parts are important.

Let us praise the Lord. Let us praise the Lord!

**Prayer:** Lord God, we praise you for the highest heavens and the waters above the skies, for the sun and moon and all the shining stars. Amen.

**Clincher:**

The sky is the daily bread of the eyes.
*—Ralph Waldo Emerson*

# 37

## Read Proverbs 15:1*

*A soft answer turns away wrath, but a harsh
word stirs up anger (Proverbs 15:1, NRSV).*

### Pain

The instant the baseball left its mark on his shoulder, Zachary felt the pain. He dropped to the ground, holding the bruised spot. "Are you okay?" the catcher asked, but Zachary couldn't answer. Stinging pain numbed his body. But he heard his coach's sympathetic voice, and he knew everything would be okay.

Words from other people affect us. Soft-spoken words often make us feel good. Harsh words usually make us feel bad. In the Hebrew language, the meaning for "harsh word" is "word of pain." Words spoken in anger do bring us pain. They make us hurt deep inside. Sometimes the hurt is much greater than a physical pain from an injury.

The words we say are like things we throw. Every word can be as soft as a pillow or as hard as a baseball. What kind of words will you throw today? Will they be words of pain or words of joy?

**Prayer:** Loving God, creator of all words, we don't always use words in the right way. Forgive us, and help us make all of our words as soft as pillows. Amen.

### Clincher:

Let the words of my mouth
and the meditation of my heart
be pleasing in your sight,
O Lord, my Rock and my Redeemer.
**—from Psalm 19:14**

# 38

## Read Proverbs 17:6*

*Children's children are a crown to the aged, and parents are the pride of their children (Proverbs 17:6).*

### Rope Bridge

Ginny and Franklin laughed at Grandpa's yellow hat. "It's my crown," he told them. "Every grandpa has a crown. Did you know that?" Grandpa said that every time he put on his yellow hat, but Ginny and Franklin never asked him what he meant.

"Hurry up, Gramps!" Ginny yelled from the bridge. "The bridge is free now. We can go across." Grandpa hurried as fast as he could to the rope bridge that stretched across the neck of the pond. The children giggled as Grandpa stomped across the swinging bridge, making it swing even more than usual.

"How does it stay up?" Franklin asked.

"Strong knots," Grandpa said, pointing to the knots in the heavy rope.

We use strong knots in many kinds of work and recreational activities. What are some ways you've seen knots being used?

Knots strengthen connections in a rope, and good relationships strengthen families. In many ways, we are tied to those in our family. All the experiences we have with each other weave together into a strong knot. There are many kinds of families, just as there are many kinds of knots, but all families are important. Our families—big or small—help each of us know who we are.

When you pray, imagine holding hands with everyone in your family, as God holds all of you in a knot of love.

**Prayer:** Dear God, thank you for putting us in families, so we can learn to love each other and to love you. Amen.

**Clincher:**
I'm not you,
You're not me,
In the same home
We will be
Family.

# 39

## Read Isaiah 9:6-7

*For to us a child is born, to us a son is given, and the government will be on his shoulders. And he will be called Wonderful Counselor, Mighty God, Everlasting Father, Prince of Peace (Isaiah 9:6).*

### Three-Leaf Clover Mystery

"Look, there's a four-leaf clover," Hennie said to Tammy. Sure enough. There it was, in a patch of clover along the bike path. They had seen many three-leaf clovers that day, but Hennie was the first to spot four leaflets together on one stem. "I used to think that three-leaf clovers were the ones that were lucky. I couldn't understand why, because they were so easy to find!" Hennie laughed. "It didn't make any sense to me."

Like the young Hennie, who tried to understand her own three-leaf clover mystery, the people in Jesus' time also struggled to understand something. Many prophets—like Isaiah—talked about the Son of God who would reign forever, but few people understood that Jesus was that person. It was hard for them to see Jesus as special. To them, he was just another three-leaf clover—the same as everyone else around them.

We know that Jesus is our "Wonderful Counselor, Mighty God, Everlasting Father, [and] Prince of Peace." Jesus is our four-leaf clover, a very special being who lives forever and who is more wonderful than we can ever imagine.

What Bible words do you use when you think about Jesus? Here are a few suggestions: Shepherd, Teacher, Savior.

**Prayer:** Dear Jesus, like a four-leaf clover, you surprise us with your wonderful presence each day. Thank you for being our Lord and Savior. Amen.

**Clincher:**

WONDERFUL COUNSELOR

**Mighty God**

EVERLASTING FATHER

Prince of Peace

# 40

# Read Isaiah 61:1-3

*The Spirit of the Lord is on me, because he has anointed me to preach good news to the poor. He has sent me to proclaim freedom for the prisoners and recovery of sight for the blind, to release the oppressed, to proclaim the year of the Lord's favor (Luke 4:18-19).*

### It's a Parade!

Sadie, Grandpa, and Aunt Billie were driving to their new house in the town where Grandpa grew up. Soon they saw crowds of people lining the streets, as if they were waiting for something to happen. "Something must be goin' on here," Aunt Billie said.

"It's a parade," yelled Sadie, who had turned around to watch, "and we're in it!" Sure enough, they had taken a wrong turn and accidentally joined a parade of floats, antique cars, and bands. Grandpa began waving to the crowd, and everyone waved back.

"Do you think they'll recognize me, after I've been gone all these years?" he asked.

Returning to the place where you grew up can be like being in a parade. People see you and wave at you. You wave back, even if you don't recognize them. For some people, going home means being like they were before. For others it means being different.

When Jesus went back to Nazareth, where he grew up, he visited the synagogue and read verses from the prophet Isaiah (Isaiah 61:1-2). Then Jesus announced to everyone in the synagogue that he was the one the Scriptures were talking about—Scriptures that had been written hundreds of years before. Jesus' trip back to his hometown began his "parade" of ministry that would last for three years.

67

God chooses us to serve, too. How will you share the good news today?

**Prayer:** Dear God, through the parade of life, help me to serve you, for you have anointed me to share the good news about Jesus. Amen.

**Clincher:**
Rise and shine, and give God the glory, glory
For the year of Jubilee.
    *—Spiritual*

# 41
## Read Daniel 1:8-17

*But Daniel resolved not to defile himself with the royal food and wine, and he asked the chief official for permission not to defile himself this way (Daniel 1:8).*

### Flood

All afternoon, Sammy and Joe watched the flooded river rise. They sat in their tree house, pretending to be Tom Sawyer and Huck Finn, and wondered where the river would take them if they jumped in.

"We could get the canoe and find out," Joe said.

"No way," Sammy said. "We'd be in big trouble then."

So they sat, their bare legs dangling, and watched the river cut its way into the bank. They talked about floating in a raft on the Mississippi and meeting dukes and kings.

The Bible tells the story of Daniel, who had even greater adventures than Tom Sawyer and Huck Finn. Captured by Nebuchadnezzar, Daniel and other Hebrews were kidnapped from their homeland and moved hundreds of miles away to the kingdom of Babylon. There they chose to serve God, even though they were given new names and trained for service in the king's palace.

Each day we make choices that tell others how we feel about God. How we spend our free time, how we talk to people, how we dress, and how we eat, all reflect what we believe about God. We can be like Daniel and his friends, who dedicated themselves to God, if we make choices that honor God. We can ask God to guide us.

**Prayer:** Dear God, please guide me in all the adventures of my life. I dedicate myself to you. Amen.

**Clincher:**
  The king ordered food
  for Daniel and friends;
  the guys turned to God
  in obedience.

# 42

# Read Daniel 4:1-3

*So Shadrach, Meshach and Abednego came out of the fire, and the satraps, prefects, governors and royal advisers crowded around them. They saw that the fire had not harmed their bodies, nor was a hair of their heads singed; their robes were not scorched, and there was no smell of fire on them (Daniel 3:26b-27).*

## Miracle

King Nebuchadnezzar was convinced that a fiery furnace was the solution to Shadrach, Meshach, and Abednego's disobedience. But he hadn't figured on a miracle from God. The three Hebrews survived the blazing furnace. It was a miracle!

We like to give reasons and explanations for everything that happens on earth, so we have a hard time understanding miracles. But we can read about miracles in both the Old and New Testaments. Matthew, Mark, Luke, and John tell about more than forty miracles that Jesus performed.

Each day God works miracles in the world. Some are almost unbelievable wonders that we know couldn't have happened without God behind them. Others seem small, and almost like accidents, but they help us know that God is still at work. Look for a miracle of God's presence today.

**Prayer:** How great are your wonders, O most high God. Your miracles show us who you are. Amen.

**Clincher:**
Three faithful guys.
A raging fire.

A furious king
Set to perspire.

God's miracle.
An angel too.
The king calls off
The barbecue.

# 43

## Read Joel 2:28-29

*I will pour out my Spirit on all people*
*(Acts 2:17a).*

### Applesauce

Ty stood over the steaming apples, smashing them through the strainer to make applesauce. He named each new kettleful after his neighbors. "There's Herb and Denise, and there's the Kang family," he said. For over an hour, Ty talked about each new kettle of apples.

"Just watch those Johnson family apples change shape before your very eyes," Ty told his brother. Sure enough, as he pushed the apples against the side of the strainer with the wooden paddle, smooth yellow sauce oozed out. "Add some sugar and we have—*dah dah dah DAH*—new applesauce!"

Many good, new things will happen to us in our lives, but the most wonderful experience of all will be when God's Spirit begins to live inside us. The prophet Joel reports God's words: "I will pour out my Spirit on all people." When God's Spirit is working through each of us, we will see greater changes than we could ever imagine. The Spirit of God will make all things—*dah dah dah DAH*—new!

Sit quietly for a few moments and imagine the warm sauce of the Spirit being poured over your head.

**Prayer:** Sweet Spirit of God, come into my heart today, and live in me forever. Amen.

### Clincher:
Today, tomorrow, and forever
God's Spirit will live in me.

73

# 44

## Read Micah 6:8*

*And what does the Lord require of you? To act justly and to love mercy and to walk humbly with your God (Micah 6:8).*

### Zoo

Emily and her uncle and aunt waited in line for the zoo to open. Finally they reached the ticket booth. They paid a fee and passed through the gate. "Let's see the baby polar bears first," said Emily.

Many places require an entrance fee. When we pay our fees, we are allowed to be there that day.

What does *God* require? In 700 B.C., when the book of Micah was written, God's people believed they needed to offer a sacrifice, as a payment for sin, before they could worship God. But God told the people, through Micah, to "act justly and to love mercy and to walk humbly with your God." We are to serve God because we love God, not to pay an entrance fee, and get into God's favor.

What do the words *justice*, *love*, and *humility* mean to you? What do they mean to God? The next time you pay an entrance fee, think about what is required to enter God's kingdom.

**Prayer:** Walk with me, Lord God, as I try to serve you. Amen.

**Clincher:**
To get past the gate
That leads into life,
Stay close to Christ
And do your best part.

# 45

# Read Matthew 1:1-17

*Thus there were fourteen generations in all from Abraham to David, fourteen from David to the exile to Babylon, and fourteen from the exile to the Christ (Matthew 1:17).*

## Toy Store

In the antique store, Naomi, her mom and grandma looked at the old toys. "You'll never guess what I played with when I was little," Grandma said. "Spools. Wooden spools. When all the sewing thread was gone from them, my mother let me play with the spools. I would color faces and hair on the spools and give each one a name, an age, and a family to live in. I spent hours playing with my spools."

Families are important. Jesus was a descendant of Abraham and lived in a family, too. He knew family histories help us understand who we are. Every family has favorite stories about persons and happenings in their family history. The stories in Jesus' family history begin with Abraham, in Genesis 11, and stretch all the way to Jesus' mother, Mary, and his earthly father, Joseph, in the New Testament.

What family stories do you like to hear? Why?

**Prayer:** Dear God, as brothers and sisters in Christ, we are part of *your* family. Teach us how to live with others in the great big family of God. Amen.

## Clincher:
The family is the nucleus of civilization.
—***Will and Ariel Durant***

75

# 46

## Read Matthew 1:18-25

*"They will call him Immanuel"—which means, "God with us" (Matthew 1:23b).*

### Camp

Taylor and his family were spending the weekend at a camp. Taylor lay in his bunk in the cabin, trying to go to sleep, but the sounds of the night kept him awake. Crickets chirped, doors slammed, an owl hooted, and a bullfrog croaked. Then he heard two coyotes, howling to each other. "Are you still here?" Taylor whispered to his dad, stretched out on the bunk below.

"Yes, I am," Dad replied. "I'll be here all night."

Most of us feel better knowing another person is with us, especially at night, in the dark. Having someone nearby comforts us and helps us feel safe.

Matthew believed the prophet Isaiah was speaking of Jesus in Isaiah 7:14. Jesus was Immanuel—"God with us"! What comfort to think of Jesus as "God with us!" He is much more than a human being who did wonderful things while he lived among us. He is God.

Think about a time when you were glad another person was with you. Think about a time when you were glad God was with you.

**Prayer:** Dear Jesus, thank you for the promise that you are Immanuel. Please live forever in our hearts. Amen.

### Clincher:

In dark of night
Or light of day,
Our God will always
With us stay.

# 47

## Read Matthew 2:1-12

*On coming to the house, the Magi saw the child with his mother Mary, and they bowed down and worshiped him. Then they opened their treasures and presented him with gifts of gold and of incense and of myrrh (Matthew 2:11).*

### Necklace

At the airport, Yuki sat next to her little friend, Andrew. "What's that?" he asked, pointing to her necklace.

"A necklace," she said.

"What color is it?" Andrew asked.

"Gold," Yuki said, as she felt the delicate chain.

"Did those guys with the star give it to you?" Andrew asked. Yuki hesitated, wondering what he meant. "You know, those wise guys that brought Jesus gold and 'cense and something else."

Yuki started laughing, but Andrew was waiting for an answer. "No, I got the necklace for my birthday," she said.

"Then those wise guys *did* give it to you. They came for Jesus' birthday too."

Andrew was talking about the magi from long ago who brought Jesus gifts fit for royalty. One of those gifts was gold. It is valuable because it never rusts or dissolves away. For years and years, gold keeps its beauty. It is one of the heaviest of all metals and was used in Bible times for making jewelry, art objects, and coins.

God sent Jesus to us as a gift of gold. Jesus is worth more than we can ever imagine. He stays with us always and makes our lives warm and beautiful.

Because of God's gift to us, we honor Jesus by giving gifts to others.

What gifts did you give or receive that remind you of Jesus?

**Prayer:** Dear Jesus, just as the magi bowed down to worship you, we offer you our prayers of praise. May our worship honor you. Amen.

**Clincher:**
The Father gave the Son,
The Son gave the Spirit.
The Spirit gives us life
So we can give the gift of love.
And the gift goes on . . .
*—Claire Cloninger and Ron Harris*

# 48

## Read Matthew 2:19-23

*After Herod died, an angel of the Lord appeared in a dream to Joseph in Egypt and said, "Get up, take the child and his mother and go" (Matthew 2:19-20a).*

### Migration

"The geese are back!" Liz yelled to her brother Marty, who was in his room. She ran up the steps and found him sitting in his closet, reading a book. "Marty. . . ," she began, but he interrupted her.

"You're never going to believe what I just read," Marty said. "Guess which bird has the longest migration route of any bird?"

"The goose?" said Liz.

"The arctic tern. It flies from the Arctic to the Antarctic Ocean every year—25,000 miles (40,000 km) round trip! And sandpipers can fly 110 miles (176 km) per hour. Songbirds migrate at night, and the white stork goes from northern Europe down into . . ."

Now Liz interrupted. "Marty, you didn't hear what I said. The geese are back!"

"Well, why didn't you tell me?" He crawled out of the closet and was down the stairs and out the front door before Liz could move.

The seasonal migrations of birds are fascinating. When the weather changes, birds begin their flight—in family groups, with other species, or alone.

Jesus' family, guided by a visit from an angel, left Egypt to return to Nazareth, where Mary and Joseph had lived before Jesus was born. We don't know if they traveled alone or with other families. We don't know if they were excited to be going home or not.

But we do know that Joseph had reasons to be worried about the trip.

Moving is a part of life, and people respond in different ways. We may be nervous, afraid, or angry. But we can put aside our worries if we trust that God is guiding us. Just as birds instinctively follow the best migration routes, we can feel God's guidance when we move.

**Prayer:** Dear God, as we move from place to place, may you guide all of our travels. Amen.

**Clincher:**
> On laisse un peu de soi-même
> En toute heure et dans tout lieu.
> (We leave behind a bit of ourselves
> Wherever we have been.)
> —*Edmond Haraucourt*

# 49

## Read Matthew 4:18-22*

*"Come, follow me," Jesus said, "and I will make you fishers of men" (Matthew 4:19).*

### Jump Rope

Jump ropes intrigued Nathan. Once, his big sister Julie had shown him cats that ran along the rope, chasing each other. They weren't really cats, but when Nathan held one end of the jump rope tight and Julie flipped the other end, the rope rippled all the way to his end. He thought he could see cats, following each other along the rope. With one flick of her wrist, Julie transformed an ordinary rope into something special.

Jesus transformed ordinary people into his special followers with one command. When he called Peter and the other disciples, they followed him and became his students. The word **disciple** means **pupil**. Following Jesus meant spending time with him and learning from him. That's what it meant to be a disciple.

We can be disciples of Jesus, too. As we follow in his footsteps, we will change from ordinary people into special people who see life in a new way. Just as Jesus called his disciples, he calls us to "leave our nets" and follow him.

Imagine you are an ordinary rope. Picture Jesus picking up the rope, and changing you into one of his followers. What kind of changes would you feel?

**Prayer:** Where you lead me, great Teacher, I will follow. Amen.

**Clincher:**
Jesus gives new meaning to Follow the Leader.

# 50

## Read Matthew 5:21-26
*Live in peace with each other (1 Thessalonians 5:13b).*

### Gecko

Thabo chased a gecko he found on the wall in the guest house. He had seen geckos before, but had never been close enough to catch one. Thabo grabbed the lizard's tail and reached for the rest of its thin-skinned body. It wasn't there! Surprised, Thabo looked up to see the rest of the gecko disappearing into a closet.

The gecko defends itself by losing its tail. When attacked, it leaves its tail behind and runs away. Later, a new tail will grow to replace the missing one.

Sometimes *we* lose our tails when we can't get along with certain people. No, we can't really lose our tails because we don't have tails. But we can lose something in the experience. Jesus talked to the disciples about how to get along with people. He said to settle arguments quickly, and compared anger to murder. Instead of running away like the gecko, we must learn to get along with others who don't agree with us. We need to talk and try to come up with good solutions.

What disagreements have you had with others? How can you keep from losing your tail, the next time you have a disagreement?

**Prayer:** God of peace and love, help us to know how to live together. Teach us your ways of peace-making. Amen.

### Clincher:

When elephants fight, it is the grass that suffers.
  —*Kikuyu proverb*

# 51
## Read Matthew 5:33-37

*Let your "Yes" be yes, and your "No," no (James 5:12b).*

**More**

Josue looked up at the hostess. She was asking him something, but this new language sounded so confusing. Was she saying, "Are you full?" He nodded his head to say "Yes." The hostess spooned more food onto his plate.

"Why did she give me more?" Josue asked his translator.

"She asked if you wanted more food, and you said you did," the translator answered.

Josue started to laugh. He shared his story, and soon everyone else was laughing, too. "I guess my 'yes' meant 'no,' " Josue said.

Sometimes we talk without knowing what we're saying, even in our own language. Sometimes we talk without thinking. In Jesus' time, people used oaths to make sure a promise was solemn and true. But some people were misusing the oaths. Jesus said we need to tell the truth at all times. When we say "yes" or "no," we should mean what we say. How would the world be different if everyone told the truth all the time? Is it possible to be loving and truthful at the same time?

**Prayer:** Dear God, help us to tell the truth, and to mean what we say. May everything we say and do be pleasing to you. Amen.

**Clincher:** It takes two to speak the truth—one to speak, and another to hear.
        —*Henry David Thoreau*

# 52
## Read Matthew 6:5-14

*And when you pray, do not keep on babbling like pagans for they think they will be heard because of their many words (Matthew 6:7).*

### Sandwich

"I just love sandwiches," said Andee, sinking her teeth into a chicken salad sandwich.

"You can thank the Earl of Sandwich," her dad said.

"Why?" Andee mumbled, trying to chew.

"He didn't want to stop his card playing to eat a meal, so he had his servants bring him beef between slices of bread. That way, he could eat and play cards at the same time. Because of him, we now have the sandwich. He actually changed the way people eat."

"Thank you, Mr. Earl of Sandwich," said Andee.

Jesus changed the way people thought about prayer. Temple prayers were no longer the only way to pray. Jesus taught his disciples to pray simply. The Lord's Prayer is the perfect example of a simple prayer.

The simple sandwich fills the need of our bodies. The simple prayer fills the need of our souls. When you eat a sandwich, think of Jesus who hears all our prayers.

**Prayer:** Dear loving Jesus, may all our prayers bring us closer to you. Amen.

### Clincher:

Day by day, dear Lord, of thee three things I pray:
to see thee more clearly,
love thee more dearly,
follow thee more nearly, day by day.
   —*St. Richard of Chichester*

# 53

## Read Matthew 7:12*

*The entire law is summed up in a single command: "Love your neighbor as yourself" (Galatians 5:14).*

### Golden Swing

"Here we go!" Caleb heard someone squeal, just as the Golden Swing amusement park ride plummeted downward. For a moment, he felt like he was hanging in air. Then the swing flew by the people on the ground and headed up in the opposite direction. It paused, then sped down and back up again.

Amusement park rides are often bigger versions of backyard play equipment. Like backyard swings, gigantic pendulums like the Golden Swing ride prove that for every action there is an equal and opposite reaction (Newton's third law of motion).

Jesus saw the same rule in everyday relationships. What you do to others, he explained, will come back to you. If you want Brian to treat you fairly, you must treat Brian fairly. If you plan to punch Jan in the nose, then you can expect Jan to punch you in the nose, too. We've given a special name to this wise saying. It's called the golden rule.

Each time you see a swing, think about the golden rule and the way your actions can come back to you. Can you remember a time when this happened?

**Prayer:** Dear God, lift me up, and let me fall into your wonderful love. Amen.

**Clincher:**

Whatever I do,
Whatever I say,
Will come back to me
In some kind of way.

85

# 54

## Read Matthew 7:24-27*

*The rain came down, the streams rose, and the winds blew and beat against the house; yet it did not fall, because it had its foundation on the rock (Matthew 7:25).*

### Toothpick House

Dion was using only drops of glue to hold his toothpick house together. Just as he added the cardboard roof, his little sister ran through the kitchen and bumped the table. Dion's house fell apart. "Oops, I'm sorry," said Kara. "Shall I help you build it again?"

"I guess so. I knew it wasn't strong, but I thought it would last longer than this! Let's use *lots* of glue this time, and put a piece of cardboard underneath." Dion and Kara laid the foundation for the second house, and added a thick layer of glue between each toothpick.

The story of the wise and foolish builders compares people to houses. It teaches us how important it is to build our lives on a good foundation, the foundation of Jesus.

Jesus holds us firm. He is the glue that runs thick and white over our lives, keeping us strong. Little drops of Jesus now and then won't be enough to hold us in a firm relationship with him. We need Jesus to coat our lives—like builders use plaster—so that we are willing to follow him in everything.

**Prayer:** Dear Jesus, I need you to be with me all the time. Please keep me strong. Amen.

**Clincher:**
The kingdom of Jesus is like the boy who used thick glue to build a toothpick house.

# 55

## Read Matthew 8:23-27

*Trust in the Lord with all your heart (Proverbs 3:5a).*

### Worried

Megan and Kris leaned against the canoe, waiting for their guide to return. They were on their third day of a weeklong canoe trip in the wilderness. "She's never taken this long before," Megan said. "Where is she?"

"I'm not worried," said Kris. "She said it would take about half an hour. We can trust her."

What things do you worry about? Often worries can take over and make it hard for us to think of anything else. We worry about robbers, accidents, storms, and wild animals. Yet we say that we trust Jesus.

When a storm pounded the disciples' boat, they begged Jesus to save them. They forgot to trust him. When Jesus calmed the wind and the waves, his miracle reminded them to trust him always.

Jesus is like a guide in the wilderness. We can trust him to help us in the stormy times in our lives. With Jesus, we can put our worries aside.

Make a list of things you worried about in the past week. Put the list inside your Bible.

**Prayer:** Dear Jesus, I will trust in you always. I give all my worries to you. Amen.

### Clincher:

There's no time like now to trust in Jesus,
No time like now to trust in my Lord,
No time like now to trust in Jesus,
Trust him and trust him
and trust him some more.

# 56

## Read Matthew 13:31-32*

*The kingdom of heaven is like a mustard seed
(Matthew 13:31).*

### Carrot Seeds

Jake spent Saturday morning working in the garden. He dropped tiny carrot seeds into a shallow ditch in the crusty soil, right next to a row of radishes just peeking through. He covered the seeds lightly with dirt. That afternoon it rained so much that water flooded his garden. Jake wondered what happened to his carrot seeds. A month later, he found carrot plants growing everywhere—in the radishes, in the flowerbed, and even in the sandpile.

Seeds surprise us. They grow in unusual places, carried by water, wind, birds, animals, and people. They're small, but the God-given energy inside them makes large plants. How and when and where the plants will grow is God's secret.

Jesus used the tiny mustard seed to teach his listeners about the surprises in God's kingdom. We find God and the church in places we could never imagine. The church has sprouted and grown in many places, all over the world.

What seeds of God are growing inside you today? Where will they take you?

**Prayer:** Dear God of people everywhere, plant us wherever we can serve you. Amen.

### Clincher:

The coconut seed and the orchid seed
Went out to play one day.

The coconut went way out to sea
And floated far away.
The orchid drifted to a branch
And rooted onto it.
The kingdom of God is planted like these
Both near and far away.

# 57
## Read Matthew 14:13-21

*Jesus replied, "They do not need to go away. You give them something to eat" (Matthew 14:16).*

### Math Problem

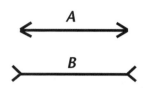

Which line is longer—line A or line B? *(Wait for response.)* Both lines are the same length, but they seem different because of the arrows at the ends. The arrows at the end of line A make the line seem shorter. The arrows at the end of line B branch out and make the line seem longer. This is called an optical illusion. Sometimes things are different from what we think we see.

The disciples looked at the crowd of people and saw a big problem. The people needed to eat, and no one could expect five loaves of bread and two fish to feed such a crowd. Jesus looked at the people and saw an opportunity. With God's help, he could feed everyone.

When you have a problem, do you see it like line A or line B? Many of us see problems the way the disciples did—like line A. We don't even try to reach out for answers. We should approach problems as Jesus did, instead, reaching out like line B.

Are the arrows at the end of your line reaching in or out? Who can you help as you reach out today?

**Prayer:** Dear God, I reach out to you today, looking for your guidance in my life. Amen.

**Clincher:**
Giving is true having.
—*Charles Haddon Spurgeon*

# 58

## Read Matthew 14:22-32

*During the fourth watch of the night Jesus went out to them, walking on the lake (Matthew 14:25).*

### Attack Cat

Annie had a big yellow cat named Hobbes, after Calvin's comic strip friend. Hobbes liked to crouch behind a rock or a tree, waiting for someone to walk past. Then he would leap out and pretend to attack, pawing the air and bouncing on his back legs, and then run up the nearest tree. Hobbes never hurt anyone, and he wasn't nearly as brave as he pretended to be. But he did like to surprise people.

We have all been surprised by someone or something. Maybe we were even afraid when a friend popped out of a closet to say, "Surprise!" What surprising experiences have you had? Were you afraid?

When Jesus walked on the water, the disciples were terrified. "Don't be afraid," Jesus said to them. He even helped Peter to walk on the water, too. With Jesus at our side, we don't have to be afraid. When Jesus is with us, we can do amazing things.

How is God telling you to be brave today?

**Prayer:** Dear Jesus, climb into my boat and help me have the courage I need today. Amen.

**Clincher:**

Fear. From a distance it is something; and nearby it is nothing.

*—Jean de La Fontaine*

# 59

## Read Matthew 18:12-14*

*He tends his flock like a shepherd: He gathers the lambs in his arms and carries them close to his heart; he gently leads those that have young (Isaiah 40:11).*

### Easter Egg

"Twenty-one . . . twenty-two . . . twenty-three. We're still missing one," Amber said. Amber and her cousins were counting the Easter eggs they had found. "Grandpa said he hid two dozen. That's twenty-four. We have to go find the last one." The cousins searched again in the tall grass and in the tulip bed. "Here it is," called Amber, holding up a purple egg. "It was under the sticker bush."

We're especially happy when we find something that was lost or hidden. No matter what it is—a piece of clothing, a kitchen tool, or a school assignment—the lost item seems more important than anything else. (Share your stories about missing things, animals, or people.)

We call Jesus the Good Shepherd, because of the lost-sheep story. Jesus cared about everyone, not just those who loved him. We are all children of God, but if we do get lost, we can know Jesus will come searching for us.

Imagine that you are all Easter eggs, scattered around during the day. Think of Jesus as the one who finds all the eggs and places them in the great big basket of God's love.

**Prayer:** Good Shepherd, as I wander about on the hills of life, I need your gentle hand to tug me back into the fold. Amen.

**Clincher:**

  I am Jesus' little lamb,
  Ever glad at heart I am;
  Jesus loves me, Jesus knows me,
  All things fair and good He shows me,
  Even calls me by my name;
  Ev'ry day He is the same.

  Safely in and out I go,
  Jesus loves and keeps me so.
  When I hunger, Jesus feeds me;
  When I thirst, my Shepherd leads me
  Where the waters softly flow,
  Where the sweetest pastures grow.

  *—Henrietta Luise von Hayn*
  *(translated by William F. Stevenson)*

# 60

## Read Matthew 20:1-16

*For the kingdom of heaven is like a landowner who went out early in the morning to hire men to work in his vineyard (Matthew 20:1).*

### Cottontails

Once there was a family of cottontail rabbits that went out to harvest their carrots. All of them were eager to fill their hillside burrow with big, crunchy carrots. After the first hour of work, the youngest rabbit said, "My tail is getting heavy. I'm done working." And he went to lie down in the lettuce patch. By the end of the second hour, the second youngest rabbit said, "My tail is getting heavy. I'm done working." And he, too, went to lie in the lettuce patch.

So it went, all day long. Every hour, another rabbit said, "My tail is getting heavy. I'm done working." At dark, the oldest of the rabbit children and the mama rabbit finished the work. Mama called her seven rabbits together and gave each one a big, crunchy carrot. The oldest rabbit started to grumble. He'd worked longer than anyone else, and he thought he should get more carrots, too. He went to find his calculator.

Many of us are like the oldest rabbit who tried to make sure he got a fair wage. We often think about money and what's fair. But the story Jesus told about the landowner and his workers is not about money, or fair pay. It's about God's generosity.

God loves us so much and is so generous that our ideas about work and rewards make as much sense as rabbits harvesting carrots. We don't earn God's love by hard work. It's there for us all the time. What's important, Jesus says, is trying to serve God however we can. We shouldn't compare ourselves with others.

The next time you eat a big, crunchy carrot, think about God's generous love for you.

**Prayer:** Dear God, thank you for stories that teach us about you. And thank you for your generous love. Amen.

**Clincher:**

# 61

## Read Matthew 22:34-40

*Love the Lord your God. . . . Love your neighbor as
yourself (Matthew 22:37-38).*

### Broken Clock

Dong . . . dong . . . dong . . . dong . . . Tony listened
as the mantle clock struck nineteen times. **Nineteen?**
Something was wrong. Tony's great-aunt Maria came
into the room. "The clock's broken," she said.

"Why don't you get it fixed?" Tony asked.

"I've tried. They don't make the parts anymore."
Tony wanted to ask why she didn't get rid of it, but he
didn't. He knew Aunt Maria would keep the two-
hundred-year-old clock as long as she could.

Family treasures stay with us. Even ones that don't
work anymore are important to many families. They
remind us of people who were close to us.

When a Pharisee asked which commandment was
the most important, Jesus gave two answers. He said
to love the Lord and to love your neighbor. These
commandments are like family treasures. They are
important truths, and unlike family treasures that can
break or wear out, these commandments will last.

What does it mean to love the Lord and to love
your neighbor as yourself?

**Prayer:** Great Teacher, I want to treasure your great
commandments today and always. Amen.

### Clincher:

It is not said that you should demand love of your
neighbor, but that you should love him.
> —*Christian Burkholder*

# 62

## Read Matthew 26:6-13

*A woman came to him with an alabaster jar of very expensive perfume, which she poured on his head as he was reclining at the table (Matthew 26:7).*

### Bakery

"What's that smell?" Rosie asked, as she and her friend Frances opened the door to the bakery.

"Rye bread and kolaces," Frances answered. "I love coming in here, just to smell the bread. When Mom buys some, then we take the smell home with us."

Some smells overpower other odors. If you walk into a bakery, the smell of bread fills the room. In a garage, the smell of oil and grease is everywhere. What kinds of smells do you smell every day? *(Pause for responses.)*

Imagine the smell in the room when the woman poured a whole jarful of expensive perfume over Jesus' head. This was her way of giving Jesus the best she had. The fragrance would have filled the entire house. The perfume was probably **spikenard** (see Mark 14:3), which had a musky odor. It was a favorite of that time. Its smell would have clung to Jesus' hair for a long time, and many others would have been able to smell it.

What we give to Jesus is like the woman's gift of perfume. When we give our best to Jesus, that gift spreads to others. We may not ever know how many people have good things happen to them because of our first gift.

May each of us serve Jesus today by sharing our best gifts with others, and may those gifts fill all the world with the fragrance of love and peace.

**Prayer:** Dear Jesus, today I give you the gifts I have to offer. Amen.

**Clincher:**
> Smoke from the fireplace,
> Aunt Darda's powder,
> Oranges just peeled,
> Sausage corn chowder,
>
> Pen full of puppies,
> Big Toby's toolbox,
> Hayfields and wheatfields and
> Fish by the boat docks.
>
> These are the smells I smell each day,
> These are the smells that won't go away,
> These are the smells I smell each day,
> Spreading their odors beyond the doorway.
>
> A lesson is learned from smells like these.
> We can reach out to others with similar ease,
> Sharing our gifts will surely please
> Jesus and God and the Spirit three.

# 63

## Read Matthew 28:16-20

*Go and make disciples of all nations, baptizing them*
*. . . and teaching them (Matthew 28:19-20).*

### Raindrops

After the rain, a puddle of water stood in the yard. Abby, wearing her old yellow raincoat and red boots, saw the sky reflected in the water and leaned down for a closer look. Then more raindrops fell, and a few of them landed in the puddle. Each drop rippled outward, connecting with others. "They're making friends," Abby exclaimed, running to the house. "Come and see the raindrops making friends!"

Jesus wanted his disciples to be like raindrops. He commanded them to go out to all people and teach them about God.

When Jesus touches our lives, he wants us to be like raindrops. He wants us to ripple outward and share the good news. When we're excited about Jesus, we will share that with other people. We want others to know how wonderful it is to have a friend like Jesus. After all, it's hard for a raindrop who loves Jesus to stay in one place.

Think about how you might be a raindrop for Jesus today. Then, start rippling!

**Prayer:** Dear Jesus, I want to be a raindrop for you. Fill me with your love as I reach out to others. Amen.

### Clincher:

Eternal life is yours. Celebrate. Don't hold this good news to yourself. Tell everyone.
—*Sally Schreiner*

99

# 64

## Read Mark 1:4-11

*It is written in Isaiah the prophet: "I will send my messenger ahead of you, who will prepare your way." . . . And so John came. (Mark 1:2,4a).*

### Train Whistle

When the new train rumbled into town for the first time, Beth heard its whistle before she saw the cars. *I've been waiting all summer for this,* she thought. She washed the sand off her feet and ran to stand near the tracks where others had gathered to see the train. The engine's long, drawn-out whistles seemed to say, "I'm coming. I'm coming." Then Beth could see the train's light, and soon the engine and cars pulled into the station, shaking the ground where she stood.

Engineers announce that a train is coming by blowing a whistle. Traffic signs, emergency sirens, and weather forecasters, too, announce the arrival of something important.

John the Baptist announced something important. He was like a train whistle when he told others about the coming of Jesus. He said, "He's coming. He's coming," to the people in Judea. When John baptized Jesus in the Jordan River, the baptism announced that Jesus' ministry was beginning.

Think about important times in your relationship with God. Are you ready to make a commitment to Christ? Are you ready to roll into God's train station and announce to God, "I'm coming, I'm coming"?

**Prayer:** Dear God, I love you, and I'm going to tell the whole world about you. Amen.

**Clincher:**
> You can tell the world about this,
> You can tell the nations about that,
> Tell them what the Master has done,
> Tell them that the Gospel has come,
> Tell them that the vict'ry's been won.
> He brought joy, joy, joy, joy,
> joy, joy into my heart.
>
> — *Bob Camp and Bob Gibson*

# 65

## Read Mark 1:35-37*

*Very early in the morning, while it was still dark,
Jesus got up, left the house and went off to a solitary
place, where he prayed (Mark 1:35).*

### Mango Tree

On his perch high up in the mango tree, Dauda bit into a juicy mango and thought about life. He was alone, his knees touching his shoulders and his arms hugging a large branch. He wiped his sticky hands on his shirt and sat for a long time—so long that the tree bark left its pattern on his bare feet. Then a clod of dirt flew by, and Dauda looked down to see his friends. They were aiming for the best mangoes and hoping to make them drop. Smiling, Dauda picked several mangoes and threw them at the boys.

Sometimes it's hard to find a quiet place to be alone. Whether we're up in a tree or down in a cellar, others can find us and interrupt us. Where is your favorite place to be alone?

Jesus liked to spend time by himself, to pray and talk with God. It was his time to be filled with God's power, the way we are filled with food each time we eat. Even though Jesus had a lot of people around him, he found quiet places where he could be with God.

Prayer is much more than just talking to God. It's being in God's presence and being filled with God's special power. It's important for each of us to find times to be with God. Climb a tree in your mind and spend time with God.

**Prayer:** Dear loving God, like Jesus, I need you and need to spend time with you. Amen.

**Clincher:**
   Up in a tree,
   Or down by the sea,
   Wherever I am,
   God comes to me.

# 66

## Read Mark 2:1-12

*Some men came, bringing to him a paralytic, carried by four of them. Since they could not get him to Jesus because of the crowd, they made an opening in the roof above Jesus and, after digging through it, lowered the mat the paralyzed man was lying on (Mark 2:3-4).*

### Rabbit in the Moon

A full moon beamed its golden face on the family as they sat outside on a warm evening. "Today's paper said the moon will keep us from seeing the meteor shower this year," Dad announced. "Too much light."

"I don't want to see the meteors anyway," said Andrea. "I don't like to stay up so late. I'd much rather just sit here and see the rabbit in the moon."

"Rabbit?" R. J. asked in disbelief. "You see a rabbit? I see a bear."

"I see a dinosaur," Kim said.

Soon the whole family was in on the friendly argument about what image they saw in the moon. "You mean to tell me," Dad said, "that I've gone through my whole life seeing a man in the moon, and it's really something else? This is unbelievable!"

Sometimes we see only what we want to see, and understand only what we want to understand. Sometimes people around us keep us from seeing and understanding the truth, just like the light from the moon kept the family from seeing the meteor shower.

Many people gathered to see Jesus and to hear his preaching. The friends of the paralyzed man believed that Jesus could heal him, and Jesus did. But others didn't believe he was God. They couldn't understand who Jesus really was.

What keeps *us* from believing in Jesus? Jesus can heal us and make us new people, if we let him.

**Prayer:** Dear Jesus, I believe that you are the Son of God. I want to see and feel you close to me always. Amen.

**Clincher:**
Summer and winter, and springtime and harvest,
sun, moon, and stars in their courses above,
join with all nature in manifold witness
to thy great faithfulness, mercy, and love.
—*Thomas O. Chisholm*

# **67**
# Read Mark 4:26-29

*[Jesus] also said. "This is what the kingdom of God is like. A man scatters seed on the ground. . . . the seed sprouts and grows, though he does not know how (Mark 4:26, 27b).*

## Wind Mystery

When Casey woke up, he heard a **whooshing** sound, and a branch from the willow tree tapping on his window. Turning over in bed, he thought about the wind and how it brushed the branch against the window. For a while the wind let up. Then it started again. *Where does the wind start?* Casey wondered. *Where does it go?*

Scientists can tell us wind speed and direction. They can also try to explain the conditions that cause the wind. But few people can explain what wind is. It's one of the mysteries of nature, like caterpillars that turn into butterflies and snakes that shed their skin.

Another mystery is the seed that sprouts and grows, even though we who plant it don't understand how. Jesus used the story of the seed to explain faith. Little by little, without us understanding how or why, our faith in God grows. Each day of each year, we learn more and more about God and the Bible. How we live changes too, as we learn what it means to follow Christ.

We are the seeds that God has planted. How will you sprout in response to God's tender care?

**Prayer:** Loving God, as I grow in my understanding of you, may I be like the seed you have filled with wonderful greatness. Amen.

**Clincher:**
Who has seen the wind?
Neither you nor I:
But when the trees bow down their heads,
The wind is passing by.
—*Christina Rossetti*

# 68

## Read Mark 9:33-35*

*Sitting down, Jesus called the Twelve and said, "If anyone wants to be first, he must be the very last, and the servant of all" (Mark 9:35).*

### Upside Down

Whitney hung upside down from the playground's highest bar. She was pretending to be the opossum she'd seen in a library book. Blood rushed to her head, and she felt dizzy at first, but then she saw children running on a brown sky, and flat white clouds holding up a blue earth. Whitney's friend, Samantha, ran up to her, and their eyes stared into each other's mouths. "Let's be first to line up, so we can get our drinks first," Samantha said. But Whitney was still upside down when the teacher's whistle blew, and she was dizzy at first, so she had to walk slowly. She and Samantha were the last to line up.

First in line for drinks, first in the race, first in the class. Everyone wants to be first. Everyone wants to be the best.

The twelve disciples wanted to be the best, too. When they argued about who was the greatest, Jesus told them his new teaching. It changed everything. "To be great," Jesus said, "you must serve others." This new teaching turned everything upside down. Serving others instead of trying to be first was one of the most important things Jesus taught his disciples.

Sometimes when we study the teachings of Jesus, we almost have to "stand on our heads," trying to understand what they mean. We have to look at things in an entirely new way, giving much more importance to helping others than to being first.

**Prayer:** Dear God, I want to live in your upside-down kingdom, serving others instead of serving myself. Amen.

**Clincher:** Which one of Jesus' teachings is hardest for you to understand?

# 69

## Read Luke 2:1-20

*(Mary) gave birth to her firstborn, a son. She wrapped him in cloths and placed him in a manger, because there was no room for them in the inn*
*(Luke 2:7).*

**Puzzle**

Here's a word puzzle. What one word can you put in front of these three words to form new words? *Place, certificate, day. (Pause for responses.)* Did you think of the word *birth*? Adding that word makes the words *birthplace, birth certificate,* and *birthday.* Can you think of other words that begin with the word *birth*?

Human beings are alike in many ways. One way we're alike is that we were all born. At some place, on a certain day, each of us was born. We may each have a birth certificate to prove it.

Jesus was born, too. He was as human as every other baby born on this earth. And he was God. Think about that. Isn't it amazing that God would become a human being? Not a grown-up human being, but a tiny baby.

The wonderful thing about Jesus is that through him, God became a person to us. We understand God better when we know God is not just some big, powerful being, far away from us. God is also very close and is a wonderful best friend. And because God did live in a human body, we know God can understand how we feel all the time!

What does it mean to you when you think of Jesus as your brother?

**Prayer:** *(in a whisper)* Thank you, Jesus, for being like me. Amen.

**Clincher:**

The virgin Mary had a baby boy . . .
The angels sang when the baby born . . .
The wise men saw when the baby born . . .
and they say that his name was Jesus.
—*West Indian carol*

# 70

## Read Luke 2:41-52

*After three days [Mary and Joseph] found [Jesus] in the temple courts, sitting among the teachers, listening to them and asking them questions (Luke 2:46).*

### Under the Pillow

Douglas was worried about the big test on Friday. He carried his science book with him constantly. He even put the book under his pillow at night. "Are you planning to dream about science?" his big brother, Jim, asked.

"No. I figure I might absorb the chapter on light waves while I'm sleeping," said Douglas.

"Do you think you'll be brighter after a week of this?" Jim teased.

As Douglas might have found out, studying the contents of the book probably helped him more than tucking it under his pillow. But each of us learns in a different way and at our own pace, and we all have favorite ways of absorbing new information. We're as different about learning as we are about eating and sleeping.

In Luke 2, we read about how Jesus learned when he was twelve. This is the only Bible story about Jesus when he was growing up. It tells us he listened to the teachers in the temple and asked them questions. By age twelve, Jesus had become so interested in religion that he missed the caravan home, and Mary and Joseph searched three days before finding him in the temple.

What new things are you learning at this point in your life? What stories of faith are important to you? How do you enjoy learning about Jesus and the Bible?

112

**Prayer:** Dear Jesus, as we sit at your feet, help us find the answers to our questions about you. Amen.

**Clincher:**

You cannot teach a man anything; you can only help him to find it within himself.

—*Galileo*

# 71

## Read Luke 4:14-21

*The Spirit of the Lord is upon me, because he has anointed me to bring good news to the poor. He has sent me to proclaim release to the captives and recovery of sight to the blind, to let the oppressed go free, to proclaim the year of the Lord's favor (Luke 4:18-19, NRSV).*

### Bear Around the Corner

"Tag me!" Rosie yelled. She was touching the tree with one arm, and stretching out the other one, hoping someone would free her from the imaginary jail. No one wanted to be caught by the pretend bear that stalked nearby. Sarah circled the tree and grabbed Rosie's hand. Rosie was free! "I'm free, I'm free. You can't get me," she sang. Holding hands, Rosie and Sarah marched confidently to the fence, where they couldn't be tagged. Then they went back to rescue other players from the bear's tree.

Rosie and Sarah were playing Bear Around the Corner. In this game, the "bear" tags players and puts them in its jail. Then other players try to release the ones who are held captive. Games like this imitate how real life is for many people. Some people are in jail in our world, either in a real jail or in a jail that is in the mind.

When Jesus started his ministry, he announced that he was chosen to minister to all people and to set them free forever.

Instead of being afraid of the Bear Around the Corner, we can look forward to seeing Jesus Around the Corner. Ask Jesus to set you free from whatever is troubling you. Then ask him to do the same for others in the world who need to be set free.

**Prayer:** Dear Jesus, I feel your gentle touch as you free me from the jail in my heart and mind. Free others who are hurting, too. Amen.

**Clincher:**
> This is the year of Jubilee.
> This is the day Christ sets us free,
> for the Spirit of God is upon him.
> Thanks be to God.
> — *Jean Janzen*

# 72

# Read Luke 10:25-37

*But a Samaritan, as he traveled, came where the man was; and when he saw him, he took pity on him (Luke 10:33).*

### An Elevator Named Henry

Once upon a time there was an elevator named Henry. He worked in a large shopping mall. Every day, Henry carried passengers up and down as they rode from floor to floor. One day, Henry woke up on the wrong side of his belt. He spent most of the morning closing the door on people and giving bumpy rides to everyone. By afternoon, Henry felt terrible; he closed the door and sulked for two hours. "Read what is written on your wall," he heard the neighboring elevator say. Henry found the words and smiled. He opened his door, greeted passengers as they stepped in, and gave them all smooth rides.

What words do you think Henry read on his elevator wall? How we treat others usually comes back to us. Sometimes we feel like ignoring other people's needs, like Henry did. But if everybody acted like that all the time, our world would be a terrible place to live.

In the parable of the good Samaritan, Jesus reminded his listeners to love all people. Everyone is our neighbor, Jesus taught us. And we are to love our neighbors as we love ourselves. That means caring for them and sharing what we have.

Plan to be a good Samaritan today. Help the first person you see who needs help.

**Prayer:** Dear God, I promise to love you, with all my heart and with all my soul and with all my strength and with all my mind, and I will love my neighbor as myself. Amen.

**Clincher:**
   He who loves brings God and the world together.
        —*Martin Buber*

# 73

# Read Luke 10:38-42

*"Martha, Martha," the Lord answered, "you are worried and upset about many things, but only one thing is needed. Mary has chosen what is better, and it will not be taken away from her" (Luke 10:41-42).*

### Clock

Kelly glanced at the clock. "Gotta go!" The words clicked from her mouth like seconds on a clock. She felt like the rabbit in Alice in Wonderland, always checking the time. Lessons, classes, games, chores. Kelly liked to do everything fast. Faster than fast. Life was a clock, and she was the second hand.

Some of us race from one activity to the next, trying to pack as much into one day as we can. Some of us like to sit, to think, and to dream.

When Jesus visited Mary and Martha, the sisters reacted to him in different ways. Martha scurried around, doing things. Then she complained to Jesus that she was stuck with all the work. Her sister, Mary, did what seemed important to her right then—listening to what Jesus had to say. Jesus told Martha not to worry about the little things but to relax and listen to others.

Each day we choose how we will spend our time. Will you take time today to sit at the feet of Jesus?

**Prayer:** Remind me, God, to choose wisely as I decide how I will spend my time. Amen.

### Clincher:
Time for work
Time for play
Time for Jesus
Every day

# 74

## Read Luke 12:22-26

*Who of you by worrying can add a single hour to his life? . . . Consider how the lilies grow. They do not labor or spin. Yet I tell you, not even Solomon in all his splendor was dressed like one of these (Luke 12:25, 27).*

### Dan-de-li-on

Riky lay on his back in the wildflower meadow with his eyes closed. Soon he felt something near his face.

"Blow, Riky, blow!" a little girl said excitedly into his ear. Riky opened his eyes and tried to focus on the white, feathery ball she held close to his face. "Blow," the girl repeated. "Then it will go POOF."

Riky sat up. "What do you call this?" Riky asked. He was still learning the English language.

"Dan-de-li-on," the girl said, emphasizing each part of the word. "Now, blow **hard**."

So Riky blew and feathery tufts took to the wind. The little girl clapped her hands and squealed in delight.

The yellow dandelion, like many other wildflowers, uses the wind to spread its seeds. Year after year, without having to think about it, it produces new flowers and seeds that grow in many places.

Jesus used a wildflower to remind his disciples to trust in God. Wildflowers and birds don't worry, so why should we? We can trust God to take care of our needs.

What do you worry about? Imagine yourself as a dandelion, when it is ready to scatter its seeds. God blows you into the world, and the Spirit-wind guides you as you float into new experiences. Wherever you land, Jesus is there to clap his hands with delight.

**Prayer:** Dear God of the flowers and the birds, I want to put my trust in you at all times. Amen.

**Clincher:**
There are two days in the week about which . . . I never worry. . . . One of these days is Yesterday. . . . And the other . . . is Tomorrow.
       *—Robert Jones Burdette*

# 75

## Read Luke 13:20-21*

*[Jesus said] "What shall I compare the kingdom of God to? It is like yeast (Luke 13:20-21a).*

### Plane Ride

Jeffrey pressed his nose against the plane's window and looked down. The city sprawled beneath him. As far as he could see, there were houses and office buildings. Cars moved like ants, on streets no wider than his finger. Jeffrey heard a man in the seat behind him say, "A hundred twenty-five years ago, there was nothin' here. Just desert. Makes you wonder how large the city'll be in another hundred years."

Cities grow. Children grow. Even ideas grow. What have you noticed growing recently?

Jesus compared the kingdom of God to yeast, that important ingredient in bread baking. Blended with warm water and mixed with flour and other ingredients, the yeast grows. It starts out tiny, then bubbles and expands until a hot oven stops its growth.

We are like yeast that is mixed with flour. All of us who love Jesus are like a big bowl full of dough, kneaded gently together by God. We're no longer single grains or individuals but a worldwide church. We're together in this bowl, growing as people of Christ.

**Prayer:** Dear God, be with us as we grow, so we can become one with those who love you. Amen.

### Clincher:

Bubbles of yeast make bread
Bubbles of Christ make the church.

# 76
# Read Luke 14:12-14

*For I was hungry and you gave me something to eat, I was thirsty and you gave me something to drink, I was a stranger and you invited me in, I needed clothes and you clothed me, I was sick and you looked after me, I was in prison and you came to visit me (Matthew 25:35-36).*

### Tea Party

Every time Erika went to her cousins' house, she had to play tea party. Abigail and Bethany dressed up in silly hats and old party dresses, set a little table with doll dishes, and served pretend cake and tea. "Who are we going to invite?" Erika asked this time. They usually invited the house cat.

"Let's ask the new neighbor—the old lady from next door who doesn't walk very good," Bethany suggested.

"But if she can't walk good, we can't invite her," Abigail said.

"Then let's take the party to her," Bethany said.

So the girls loaded their party things into the doll carriage, pushed it next door, and rang the doorbell. "Want to join our tea party?" Bethany asked.

Jesus wants us to be concerned about all people, not just those we know well, like our relatives and friends. Some people can't help themselves, and need our special care.

Let's think of ourselves as plates, loaded with pretend cake that we can serve to people who need our help. We can invite guests into our homes or take the party to them. Either way, when we're serving them, we're serving God!

**Prayer:** Dear God, I'm wearing my party hat and party clothes. I'm ready to serve you in any way I can. Amen.

**Clincher:**

Wherever there is a human being, there is an opportunity for a kindness.

—*Lucius Annaeus Seneca*

# 77

# Read Luke 17:11-16

*One of [the lepers], when he saw he was healed, came back, praising God in a loud voice. He threw himself at Jesus' feet and thanked him (Luke 17:15-16a).*

## Drop the Handkerchief

"We're going to play Drop the Handkerchief a new way," announced the leader. "The person who's 'it' drops the handkerchief behind someone, as usual. Then these two run in opposite directions around the circle, until they meet. They must stop, shake hands, and say, 'Pleased to meet you. Thank you very much.' Then they keep on running, to see who can get to the open spot in the circle first. Any questions?"

"What happens if you forget to say 'thank you'?" Luke asked.

"We'll remind you until you do," the leader said. "You won't forget."

In real life, we often forget to say thank you. The words are so simple we forget how important they are. We say thank you to politely show our gratitude for something someone has done for us. "Thank you" tells others how we feel inside.

Even in Jesus' day people forgot to say, "Thank you." Jesus healed ten people who had a serious skin disease called leprosy, and only one of them returned to thank him. Jesus wondered what happened to the others.

Saying thank you is always important—whether we're saying it to other people or to God. Close your eyes now and imagine God running up to you as you say, "Thank you very much. Thank you very much."

**Prayer:** Dear Jesus, I bow humbly before you, to thank you for everything you have done for me. Help me to remember to tell others thanks when they do nice things for me, too. Amen.

**Clincher:**
Gratitude is the heart's memory.
—*French proverb*

# 78

## Read Luke 18:15-17

*And [Jesus] took the children in his arms, put his hands on them and blessed them (Mark 10:16).*

### Toads

"Look at all the toads!" Christy exclaimed, as the family pitched their tent. "Come here, little toadies. Come here." Gently catching the little toads, Christy loaded them in her cap and her shoes. When she had more than she could carry, she went back to her family and announced, "I'm going to take them all home."

"No, you're not," said her big brother.

"Yes, I am, because I love every single one of them."

Sometimes our family and friends surprise us with the things they like. What are your favorite members of the animal kingdom?

Jesus surprised his disciples by welcoming children. He didn't want them to turn away the parents who were bringing babies to him. He held the children in his arms. He showed them the kind of love he wanted his disciples to have for people of all ages.

We need to remember that Jesus always welcomes us into his arms. It's wonderful to be with God and to feel God's acceptance—whether we're toads or humans!

**Prayer:** Dear Jesus, friend of all, may we feel your arms wrapping around us, in love and acceptance. Amen.

### Clincher:

Jesus, loving Lord;
Jesus, strength and stay,
in your mercy bless us all
and keep us night and day.
    —*A blessing from India*

# 79

## Read Luke 19:1-10

*Jesus . . . looked up and said . . , "Zacchaeus, come down immediately. I must stay at your house today"*
*(Luke 19:5).*

**Keys**

In the cellar of the old house, Nick spotted a pile of old keys. "It's a treasure!" he called to his brothers. "Let's see if these old keys fit the attic door Mom's been trying to open." The boys climbed out of the cellar, dashed up the porch steps, and into the house. They ran up two flights of wooden steps to the attic. Nick stuck the biggest key in the lock, turned it, and heard a click. "It works," he said. The attic door swung open to reveal old toys, left many years earlier by another owner. "Wow!" the boys yelled.

When Jesus went to Jericho, he met a tax collector named Zacchaeus in a most unusual place. Jesus offered him the key to his kingdom. "Come on down, Zacchaeus," Jesus said. "I'm going to visit at your house today." Zacchaeus accepted Jesus' offer. He asked Jesus to unlock the door to his heart so he could become a new person.

Are you sitting up in a tree, waiting for Jesus to talk to you? Exciting things happen when Jesus is a part of our lives. It's Jesus who can open new doors for us, and when he does, we will yell, "Wow!"

**Prayer:** Dear Jesus, I welcome you into my heart today. Amen.

**Clincher:**
Followers from A to Z
Know that Jesus is the key.

# 80

## Read Luke 19:28-38
*"Blessed is he who comes in the name of the Lord!"*
*(Psalm 118:26a).*

### Dirty Fingernails

"Now when we eat at Great-grandmother's house, please be on your best behavior," said Alex's mom, but she didn't need to remind him. He knew the rules. Cap off; napkin on the lap; elbows off the table; say "Yes, please" and "No, thank you;" and do not stare at his reflection in the white plates.

But this time, Great-grandmother had set the table with the glass plates she saved for special guests. Alex slipped his fingers under the edge of his plate, and through the fancy flowers and leaves cut into the glass design, he saw his dirty fingernails.

Jesus rode into Jerusalem on the back of a donkey. He rode like a king, receiving honor and praise from the crowd. They threw down their cloaks, as if they were throwing out the red carpet for an earthly ruler. They knew Jesus was special, and they wanted to show him. And Jesus didn't care if any of them had dirt under their fingernails.

Jesus accepts us, even with dirty fingernails, feet, or faces. He came for all of us. Whether we sit at the grandest table with the fanciest dishes or at the simplest table with only one bowl, Jesus loves us all. Whoever we are and wherever we are, we can shout praises to our God, who is king of our lives.

**Prayer:** Blessed are you, King Jesus. We bow down to you in praise and honor. Amen.

**Clincher:**

Can I ride with you on the donkey, King Jesus?
Can I ride with you on the donkey today?
I'll sit right behind you and lean on your back.
Can I ride with you on the donkey today?

# 81

## Read Luke 21:1-4

*God loves a cheerful giver (2 Corinthians 9:7b).*

### Watermelon

On a hot day, Susannah and her neighbor Lisa sat on the front porch, eating watermelon. Sticky, pink juice dribbled down their chins and arms, stained their clothes, and ended in a puddle on the ground. Flies and ants were starting to gather. "Want another piece?" Susannah asked. Lisa nodded. Susannah ran into the house, leaving a trail of watermelon juice. "I offered Lisa another piece of melon," Susannah whispered to the babysitter. "I said we have enough. Do we?"

"There's only one piece left," Maggie said.

"I'll let Lisa have it," Susannah said, carrying the last piece to her friend.

Jesus was pleased with the woman who put two small coins in the temple treasury. He knew she had given all she had. The kind of coins or the amount of the gift didn't matter.

What do you have to give to Jesus? Sharing what you have is one kind of gift. Sharing your talents is a gift, too. Set aside a time to share with someone else. May your gift be as sweet as the juice of a watermelon.

**Prayer:** Holy Jesus, bless these gifts that we offer to you. Amen.

### Clincher:

Grant us, Lord, the grace of giving,
with a spirit large and free,
that ourselves and all our living
we may offer unto thee.
    *—Anonymous*

# 82

## Read Luke 22:8, 14-20

*And [Jesus] took bread, gave thanks and broke it, and gave it to [the disciples], saying, "This is my body given for you; do this in remembrance of me" (Luke 22:19).*

### Hand Writing

"What are you writing on your hand this time?" Carmen asked Willie.

"Nothing," he said.

"Let me see, please," Carmen begged. Willie showed her his hand. He had written the letters P, H, B on it.

"What do those stand for?" Carmen asked.

"Play, horn, book," he said. "Memorize play lines, horn lesson tomorrow, and take book back to library."

"And this'll help you remember?"

"That's right. My grandma always makes lists, but then she forgets where she put them. I've never lost my hand yet!"

We use different ways to help us remember things. Sometimes we write notes to ourselves or tie strings on our fingers. What tricks have helped you to remember?

Jesus knew he was leaving. At his last meal with his disciples, he used the bread and the cup as symbols to help his followers remember him. Today we still use these two symbols to remember Jesus. They remind us of our relationship with him and with each other. These symbols are important to all people around the world who are followers of Christ.

Think about what objects or words you use to remember Jesus. What symbols do you have to remind you of Christ in the place you live?

**Prayer:** Dear Jesus, our Teacher, we give you thanks for the bread and for the cup. Amen.

**Clincher:**
I come with joy to meet my Lord,
forgiven, loved, and free,
in awe and wonder to recall
his life laid down for me . . .
I come with Christians far and near
to find, as all are fed,
the new community of love
in Christ's communion bread.
    *—Brian Wren*

# 83

## Read Luke 24:1-12

*[Jesus said], "On the third day [the Son of Man]*
*will rise again (Luke 18:33).*

**Swing**

The chain on the swing creaked. Jana sat on the seat and kept winding. She wanted the best spin possible. As soon as her toes could no longer touch the ground, the swing would fly into the spin. She saw her cat, perched on the rock by the fence.

"I'm flying, Sunshine!" she yelled as she leaned into the spin. She looked at the ground, watching the small stones become circular patterns. For a few seconds, as the spin was ending, the swing spun faster. When it rocked to a stop, Jana's head was still spinning. She looked for Sunshine, but the cat was gone.

Jesus' followers must have felt like their heads were spinning. They weren't sure what they had seen. They thought Jesus had died and his body had been placed in the tomb, but now they weren't sure. The stone was rolled away from the tomb's entrance. Jesus' body was gone. Only the strips of linen that had wrapped his body were still there. They saw angels, who told them Jesus had risen from the dead. It was confusing and wonderful at the same time. Things like this couldn't happen!

But it did happen. As followers of Christ, we believe that he died and rose again. We worship the living Christ. He sets our hearts spinning in a wonderful way. And even though we don't see him, we know he is near.

**Prayer:** Dear Jesus, you are alive, and because of you, we too can live forever. Amen.

133

**Clincher:**
>I know we spin on earth
>beneath a dancing sky,
>I hear a word from God
>that frees us all to fly . . .
>For I believe that Christ
>is changing ev'rything.
>>—*Norman C. Habel*

# 84

## Read Luke 24:13-16, 30-31

*Then their eyes were opened and they recognized him, and he disappeared from their sight (Luke 24:31).*

**Fog**

Thick fog hung over Ramon and Sandy as they followed the path to the bus stop. They could hear the lake water lapping along the shore. "Pea soup," Ramon muttered. "The fog's as thick as pea soup."

Sandy wiped the mist off his glasses. He wanted to ask Ramon what pea soup was, but the morning seemed too quiet for talk. They reached the bus stop just in time to catch their bus. The driver asked, "Did you two see the sunrise, or did you have your eyes stuck to the ground?" Sandy and Ramon looked out the window. Sure enough, a sliver of sun peeked out from under the fog, speckling the lake with shades of orange. "Good morning, Jesus," Sandy heard the driver say.

The two disciples on the road to Emmaus seemed to have their eyes covered with fog. The risen Jesus walked with them part of the seven miles from Jerusalem. He even joined them for a meal, but they didn't recognize him until he broke the bread. Then, as soon as they knew who he was, he disappeared. What a surprise! He was with them and they didn't know him. Then suddenly, he was gone.

We wonder about Jesus, too. Who is this person? Is he God or human? How can we be sure Jesus is with us all the time if we can't see him?

What questions would you like to ask Jesus right now?

**Prayer:** Jesus of Nazareth, Friend and Comforter, as I walk through each day, help me to realize you are with me. Amen.

**Clincher:**
So preoccupied with
human thoughts,
we never dreamt
the man who died
was walking with us
how often will he walk with us
on the road?
—*Yorifumi Yaguchi*

# 85

## Read Luke 24:50-53

*He was taken up before their very eyes, and a cloud hid him from their sight (Acts 1:9).*

**Candles**

The glow from the birthday candles lit Erin's face. She leaned forward, took a big breath, and blew as hard as she could. The candles flickered out and then flamed up again. "Are these some of those candles you can't blow out?" Erin asked. Her family laughed. Erin blew again and again, and still the candles stayed lit. "Do you want me to keep blowing out my candles all year long?"

Jesus is like a candle that won't blow out. His light will stay lit forever. That's what his followers were celebrating when they returned to Jerusalem after he ascended into heaven. Jesus had proven to them that he had power over death, that he would live forever. They really did have something to celebrate.

Living with Jesus is one big celebration. How does your family like to celebrate special events? That's the kind of celebrating you can do every day when you feel Jesus living inside you. Light the candles, sing songs of joy, and have a party with Jesus!

**Prayer:** We praise you, God, for our risen Lord who ascended into heaven. We worship you with joy. Amen.

**Clincher:**
Something to celebrate.
Something to cheer.
Something to sing
'Cause Jesus is near.

Lift up your hands
and clap them around.
Lift up your feet
and stomp on the ground.

Something to celebrate.
Something to cheer.
Something to sing
'Cause Jesus is near.

# 86
## Read John 10:1-5, 14
*[The shepherd] calls his own sheep
by name and leads them out (John 10:3b).*

### Pigs
"Deirdre, do you want to call the pigs?" asked the farmer. He was carrying buckets of feed to the hog pen. Deirdre stared at him, her eyes wide open. She didn't know how to call the pigs. It was her first day ever on a farm.

She walked to the fence and yelled as loud as she could. "Come here, piggy, piggy!" The pigs didn't move. "Why don't they come?"

The farmer smiled. He climbed over the fence, banged his hand on the bucket, and hollered, "Come, pig, pig, pig." The sows got up and ran for the feed. "I played a trick on you, Deirdre," the farmer said. "The pigs know my voice, and they know the bucket."

Farm animals know the farmer. The farmer knows each of the animals, too, by the way they look, the sounds they make, or the way they act.

Jesus knows us by name. We are important to God. When God calls us, we respond. What God offers us is like a big bucket of feed, overflowing with goodness.

How does it make you feel to know God knows you by name? How will you respond to God's call today?

**Prayer:** Good Farmer God, I want to follow your voice and to feel you with me throughout today. Amen.

### Clincher:
Obey my voice and I will be your God and ye shall be my people.                    *—from Jeremiah 7:23*

# 87

## Read John 21:1-14

*Early in the morning, Jesus stood on the shore, but the disciples did not realize that it was Jesus (John 21:4).*

### Dancing Mooses

Janie was lying in bed when she heard her little sister walk to the window in the upstairs hall. "What are you doing?" she called.

"I'm looking for the dancing mooses I saw last night," Kara called back. Janie crawled out of bed. *Moose don't live here,* she thought. "There they are again," Kara exclaimed. "See, under the tree?" Janie looked, too. A full moon shone through the elm branches, creating a design on the ground.

"Those aren't moose. That's just shadows from the tree. The wind is blowing the leaves."

"No, it's mooses," Kara insisted. "I see them."

Kara saw tree shadows in her backyard, and the disciples saw Jesus on the shore. Neither Kara nor the disciples understood what they were seeing.

There are times when we don't see Jesus. His Spirit might be close to us, but we only know it when a miracle happens. Then we react like Peter did when he jumped into the water, eagerly reaching for Jesus.

Look for opportunities to be with Jesus today. Spend time with him while you read your Bible or talk with a neighbor. Where do you go to search for Jesus? With Jesus nearby, you can expect to catch the Spirit of God wherever you throw out your net.

**Prayer:** Dear Jesus, thank you for your invitation to spend time with you. Amen.

**Clincher:**
The time to be happy is now,
The place to be happy is here,
The way to be happy is to make others so.
*—Robert Green Ingersoll*

# 88

## Read Acts 2:42-47

*Every day they continued to meet together in the temple courts. They broke bread in their homes and ate together with glad and sincere hearts (Acts 2:46).*

### Honey

The honey oozed over the crust of Faith's bread before she could take one bite. It dribbled down her fingers and onto her arm. She tried to wipe it with her napkin, but the napkin stuck to her arm. When her brother, at the other end of the table, asked her to pass the honey, she grabbed the jar with her sticky hand. All the way down the table, the jar turned people's smooth hands into sticky ones.

The followers of Christ stuck together. They ate together. They prayed together. They studied together. They shared everything they had. And because they loved each other, more and more people joined the group.

We, too, should stick together with other Christians. What are your favorite ways to enjoy being with others who love Jesus? Find some time today to share experiences with another follower of Christ. When you do, think of yourself as a honey bee for Christ.

**Prayer:** Dear Jesus, thank you for sweet times that I can spend with others who love you. Amen.

### Clincher:

To get the full value of joy, you must have someone to divide it with.
*—Mark Twain*

# 89

## Read Acts 8:26-31, 35

*Then Philip began with that very passage of Scripture and told [the Ethiopian] the good news about Jesus (Acts 8:35).*

### Directions

"Can you give us directions, please?" asked Mikias' older brother. Half asleep, Mikias strained to hear more. Everyone else in the car was quiet. *They must be sleeping,* he thought. He heard his brother again.

"We're trying to reach the Main Road Guest House." Mikias listened hard, so he could help his brother find the way. "This road will take you there," a man's voice answered. "Go past the new market and cross the river bridge. The guest house is right by the waterfall." Mikias' brother said thanks, and the car pulled away.

Have you ever been lost? Who helped you find your way?

The man from Ethiopia was lost. He needed someone to help him understand the Scripture. Philip helped the man find his way by telling him the good news about Jesus.

Hearing about Jesus is good news for all of us. The stories in the Bible give us direction; they help us know which road to take when we feel lost. But some parts of the Bible are hard to understand. That's when we need someone to help us find the way.

Who helps you understand the stories of the Bible? Who has brought you the good news about Jesus?

**Prayer:** Thank you, dear Jesus, for the Bible and for the people who have helped me know about you. Amen.

**Clincher:**
Just follow the Bible.
Just follow our Lord.
We have direction
When we read God's Word.

# 90
## Read Acts 16:13-15

*One of those listening was a woman named Lydia, a dealer in purple cloth. . . . The Lord opened her heart to respond to Paul's message (Acts 16:14).*

### Grape Juice

Whenever Susanna drank grape juice for breakfast, she wore a grape juice smile all day. She liked grape juice so much that when she tipped the glass and leaned back her head, extra juice stained the skin around her top lip. Her dad said, "You've got a mustache." Her big sister said, "Go wash your face," but Susanna would forget. Whenever anyone said something about the stain on her face, she would say, "This is my grape juice smile."

Fabric dyes change the color of cloth, just like grape juice stains the face. When the dye soaks into the fabric, it stays for a long time.

Lydia, one of the women Paul met outside the city of Philippi, knew all about dyed cloth. Her city was famous for its purple dye, and Lydia sold purple cloth. But Lydia also knew about the changes that happen in people's hearts when they respond to the message about Christ. The changes that made her a new person stayed with her for a long time.

When we believe in Jesus Christ, things change for us. One of those changes is that we feel happier inside. Our happiness shows, and we wear Jesus smiles for a long time.

**Prayer:** Dear God, make me a new person—inside and out. Amen.

145

**Clincher:**
I have a Jesus smile that spreads across my face.
I have a Jesus smile I know I won't erase
'Cause Jesus lives inside me
And all the time he guides me.
I have a Jesus smile that I never will replace.

# 91

## Read Romans 12:4-8

*We have different gifts, according to the grace given us (Romans 12:6).*

### Flat Tires

Flat. Both tires on Tony's bike were flat. The black rubber sagged against the ground, like loose skin on an old dog's belly. He wouldn't be able to ride to his friend's house. Without air in the tires, Tony's bike was useless.

Just then Marcos rode up on his bike. "Ready to go?" he asked.

"Both tires are flat," Tony muttered. "I don't know what to do."

"I'll help you fix them," Marcos said. "I know how to do that."

All of us have special, God-given gifts we can use to help others. That's called sharing. Sometimes we share easily, without thinking about it. Marcos knew Tony needed help. Right away he offered to help him. He knew how to fix tires, and Tony didn't.

If God gave everyone the same gifts, our world would be boring. The person who wrote Romans knew how important it is to have differences in our world and in our churches. Think about all the different gifts God has given us. Without the special gifts different people bring, our churches would work as well as two flat bike tires.

What things can you do well? What could you offer to do for your church?

**Prayer:** Dear God, thank you for the special gifts you give. Thank you for making them different. Amen.

147

**Clincher:**

There are many gifts, but the same Spirit.
There are many works, but the same God,
And the Spirit gives each as it chooses.
Praise the Lord. Praise God.
*—Patricia Shelly*

# 92

# Read Romans 12:15-18

*Live at peace with everyone (Romans 12:18b).*

### Volcano

"How do I get it to stop?" Hannah yelled. Her homemade volcano was erupting onto the floor of the kitchen. "Help! Help!"

Hannah's dad ran to help. He saw the box of baking soda and the jar of vinegar near the erupting volcano. "Add some water," he said. So Hannah doused her science experiment with water. Almost immediately the bubbles disappeared. Hannah sighed with relief, and looked at Dad. He was smiling. "I didn't know baking soda and vinegar would blow up like that," Hannah admitted.

Sometimes we act like volcanoes. It's easy to erupt when we're around certain people. We may be tempted to argue or fight, making mountains out of anthills. Romans 12, verse 18, tells us to "live at peace with everyone." We need to look for ways to make peace and to disagree with each other with an attitude of love.

If you start getting angry and erupting like a volcano, pray that God will douse you with the water of peace. Then think of a way to try to get along.

**Prayer:** Dear God, teach me how to live at peace with everyone. Amen.

**Clincher:** When you feel like boiling over, turn down the heat.

# 93
# Read 1 Corinthians 10:23-24

*Each of you should look not only to your
own interests, but also to the interests of others
(Philippians 2:4).*

### Pyramids

In the gym, Danae felt a knee dig into her back. Then a hand pushed into her shoulder blade. Looking down at the mat, she felt more weight on top of her, and knew another person was climbing on top of the human pyramid. *Just one more person,* Danae thought, *and our pyramid will be finished.* The gymnasts tottered and the pyramid swayed for a second, as the top person climbed up. Then someone yelled, "You did it! Hold it—it looks great!"

Paul encouraged the church in Corinth to be concerned about the good of others. Paul wanted the followers of Christ to be examples for non-Christians. What we do, Paul wrote, should bring glory to God (1 Corinthians 10:31).

Building human pyramids is like building human relationships. Sometimes we hold others up; other times they hold us up. It feels good to be part of a group that supports each other. And it's nice to know we have friends and family who can help us make decisions. With God encouraging us and others caring about us, we may find ourselves building human pyramids that stretch all around the world and all the way to heaven!

When has someone encouraged you?

**Prayer:** Dear Jesus, I want to build others up, like Paul, and help them learn about you. Amen.

**Clincher:**

I am
only one,
But still I am one.
I cannot do everything,
But still I can do something;
And because I cannot do everything
I will not refuse to do the something that I can do.

*—Edward Everett Hale*

# 94

## Read 2 Corinthians 5:17

*So if anyone is in Christ, there is a new creation: everything old has passed away; see, everything has become new! (2 Corinthians 5:17, NRSV).*

### Paint

Tania dipped her paintbrush into fresh paint and dabbed it on the wall. She loved the smell of paint and how it made her bedroom feel new. Eagerly she brushed over some fingerprints, and over pencil marks that read, "I hate everything!" ***Why did I ever write that?*** Tania wondered. She couldn't remember. In an hour, she stepped back to look at the painted walls. The smudges and scuff marks were gone. It seemed like a new room.

When we learn to know Christ, we are new creatures. Everything about us changes for the good. Different things seem important to us. The desire to be rich and powerful, for example, might be replaced with wanting to love and serve others.

With Jesus in our hearts, we're like a freshly painted room. We see things and people in a new light. Our dirty smudges are gone, and the holes and dents are smoothed over by Jesus' love. What is one thing you would like to have Jesus change about you?

**Prayer:** Dear Jesus, I am a new creation because of you. Thank you. Amen.

### Clincher:

New earth, heavens new, Spirit of God moving;
New seed, creatures new, Spirit of life moving . . .
Sing a new song to the One who has said,
"Behold, I make all things new."
—*Harris J. Loewen*

# 95

## Read Galatians 5:22-23*

*But the fruit of the Spirit is love, joy, peace, patience, kindness, goodness, faithfulness, gentleness and self-control (Galatians 5:22-23a).*

### Whistle

"Listen, Uncle Charlie!" Evan exclaimed. His uncle was pruning fruit trees in the orchard. He watched as Evan puckered his lips, took a big breath, and blew out the air. A long whistle eased out of his mouth.

"How'd you learn to do that?" Uncle Charlie asked.

"One day it just came, that's all," Evan said.

Sometimes the best parts of life seem to just happen. Suddenly we realize we are controlling a nasty temper or being patient, when we couldn't do it before. These are some of the fruits of the Spirit. Good things happen when we have committed our lives to Jesus. Love, joy, peace, and all the other good fruits come from God's Spirit inside us. We can't go out and buy them, like fruits from an orchard. They happen in our lives because we have said "yes" to Jesus.

Whistle a thank you to Jesus for the special gifts that grow in our hearts when we offer ourselves to him.

**Prayer:** Thank you, Jesus, for the blessings you have spread through my life. Help me to share your love with those around me. Amen.

**Clincher:**
Seek ye first the kingdom of God
and his righteousness,
And all these things shall be added unto you,
Allelu, Alleluia.
—*song based on Matthew 6:33*

# 96

## Read Philippians 4:4-7

*Rejoice in the Lord always. I will say it again:*
*Rejoice! (Philippians 4:4).*

### Studying

Polly lay on the floor, with her feet in the air and her head buried in her math textbook. She was finishing her homework on multiplying fractions. ***Grandpa would say I should sit at the table to study,*** Polly thought, ***and Mom would tell me to turn off the radio.*** But Polly was convinced she could study in any position, and she didn't care if the radio was playing loud music.

How do you like to study or read?

However you do it, you should take Paul's advice to the people in Philippi: rejoice always. In every kind of learning situation, we are to rejoice. With all kinds of people around us, we are to rejoice. Even when we are tired, sad, worried, angry, or scared, we should rejoice.

When you start each new day, take Paul's advice. Instead of complaining about math problems or doctor appointments, rejoice in the Lord and kick up your heels in celebration.

**Prayer:** Dear God, I worship you, with a smile on my face and with joy in my heart. Amen.

### Clincher:

There is . . . more Christianity in a smile than there is in a frown.
*—Sallie Kniesly*

# **97**

## Read Colossians 3:15-17

*Let the peace of Christ rule in your hearts, since as members of one body you were called to peace. And be thankful (Colossians 3:15).*

### Library

Levi opened the door to the library. *It always feels so peaceful inside,* he thought. People sat reading among stacks of books. The librarian talked quietly with a person at the checkout desk. Levi dropped a book in the slot and headed off to find another one. As he looked at the books in the fiction section, he overheard a child in the next aisle. "The librarian knows where all the books are," the child said. "Is the librarian God?" Levi smiled. *If God were the librarian, and I were a book,* he wondered, *what section would I be in?*

In his letter to the Colossians, Paul encouraged the believers to live in peace with those around them. He believed that love binds everyone together in perfect unity.

In some ways, Christians are like books in a library. We share space with others who are a lot like us, and with others who are different. Some of our favorite friends are far away, but we are bound together because we belong to the same body—the church. Over all of us is Christ, the great librarian, who guides our comings and goings and helps us live together in peace.

The next time you see a library, think about Christ's followers who are bound to others in Christian love.

**Prayer:** Loving Christ, we bow before you to thank you for your presence. May you bring peace to our lives. Amen.

**Clincher:**
Bind us together, Lord,
bind us together
with cords that cannot be broken.
Bind us together, Lord,
bind us together, Lord,
bind us together in love.
—*Bob Gillman*

# 98

## Read Titus 3:1-2

*Remind [the people] . . . to speak evil of no one, to avoid quarreling, to be gentle, and to show every courtesy to everyone (Titus 3:2, NRSV).*

### Antonyms

You know what *antonyms* are. Even if you've never heard of them, you use them every day. Antonyms are words that are opposites—like big and little, happy and sad. Here are some for you to figure out *(pause for response after each word):* young *(old),* more *(less),* start *(stop),* dry *(wet),* dark *(light).*

Think of antonyms for these words from Titus: remind, obedient, good, quarreling, gentle, show, courtesy, everyone. Sometimes it's fun to look at a Bible verse and figure out what it does *not* say. The Bible does not tell us to be disobedient, to be mean, or to push people out of our way. We should be kind and courteous to everyone—including those people who are different from us.

Think of someone who is different from you. You may have a hard time getting along with that person. When you see that person or think about him or her today, remember these words written by Paul many years ago. "Speak evil of no one, . . . avoid quarreling, . . . be gentle, . . . and show every courtesy to everyone."

**Prayer:** Help us to get along with all people, O God. Amen.

**Clincher:**
May the Great Mystery make sunrise in your heart.
    *—a Sioux blessing*

158

# 99
## Read 1 Peter 4:10-11*

*Serve one another with whatever gift each of you has received (1 Peter 4:10b, NRSV).*

**Sweat**

Beads of sweat dripped off Lauren's forehead. Her hair felt glued to her scalp. She had never felt this hot before. Just when she needed the electricity most, it had gone off. A fan would feel so good. Lauren's next-door neighbor saw her sitting beneath a tree, trying to stay out of the scorching sun.

"I'll show you how to make a paper fan," Martha said. "This is how we stayed cool when I was little." She folded a paper back and forth so it became one narrow strip; then she turned it into a fan for Lauren.

If you've made a fan out of paper, you may have noticed it can push the air in several directions. Usually more than one person can feel the breeze it makes.

That's what happens with gifts from God. If we use them as God wants, other people benefit from them, too. If God has given you the gift of singing, others can hear you and share in your gift.

When you see a fan, think about spreading God's goodness, by using the gifts God has given you.

**Prayer:** Thank you, generous God, for the gifts you have given me. Remind me to use them to serve others faithfully. Amen.

**Clincher:**
This little light of mine,
I'm gonna let it shine.
　　　*—Traditional*

159

# 100
## Read 1 John 3:16-18

*Dear children, let us not love with words or tongue but with actions and in truth (1 John 3:18).*

### Charades

"Okay, everybody, I'm ready to start," Hans said. "Guess who I am." Hans' friends watched as he slid his fingers over his hair, pretended to pick something up, and started skipping around the room.

"He's got something on his head and he's going somewhere. You're skipping. That's it—skip!" one of them yelled. But Hans kept on acting, pretending to open a door and walk through it.

"I've got it! You have your briefcase and you're going to work." But that person was wrong, too. For a long time, Hans repeated the charade. Finally, he acted like he was lying in bed and had pointed ears.

"The wolf!" another person yelled. "It's the wolf in Grandma's bed. You're Little Red Riding Hood!"

Some of us do a good job of acting. We like to play games that let us pretend.

The Bible tells us that it's important to act out what we believe. It's easier to tell others that we love them, but expressing love through our actions is more important. Without actions, our words of love don't mean anything.

Little Red Riding Hood acted out her love for her grandmother. Who are your favorite story characters? Do any of them act out their love?

Pretend to be Little Red Riding Hood and do something nice for someone today. (Don't worry about any wolves.)

**Prayer:** Dear Jesus, remind me to serve others always. Amen.

**Clincher:** We know what a person thinks, not when he tells us what he thinks, but by his actions.
—*Isaac Bashevis Singer*

# **101**

## Read Jude 1:24-25

*To him who is able to keep you from falling and to
present you before his glorious presence without fault
and with great joy—to the only God our Savior be glory,
majesty, power and authority, through Jesus Christ our
Lord, before all ages, now and forevermore! Amen
(Jude 1:24-25).*

### Benediction

Click. Maria watched her mother's hand as it
turned the key to lock the door to the store. Maria
remembered what Mom had told the last customer.
"Closing the door is like the benediction to the day."

"What did you mean about the benediction?"
Maria asked, as they walked home. "Isn't that what
happens at the end of the church service?"

"Well, when I close up the store," Mom answered,
"I think of all the good people I've met that day, and
I kind of take their spirits home with me. When I
leave church, I take the spirit of the church with me.
I know God is with me everywhere."

In the last two verses of Jude, we read one of the
great benedictions, or closing prayers, found in the
New Testament. It reminds us that the Spirit of God
our Savior is with us all the time. Because of that, we
can be especially happy. Our glorious God is alive
and with us, and we, like all God's people everywhere, will live forever in the great benediction of
God's love.

**Prayer:** May God's Spirit, locked in your heart by
the power of love, go with you always. Amen.

**Clincher:**

I'll spread God's peace
to the world,
with·conviction,
And share God's love
in a great benediction.

# Scripture Index

# Subject Index

*(Listed by Number of Devotional)*

167

# Quoted Materials

#3      ***The Reader's Digest Great Encyclopedic Dictionary***, The Reader's Digest Association, Inc., 1966

#5, #6    ***Lewis C. Henry's Five Thousand Quotations for All Occasions,*** Doubleday & Company, Inc., 1945

#10     ***Familiar Quotations***, by John Bartlett

#16, #17 Excerpted by permission from ***Readings from Mennonite Writings New & Old*** by Craig Haas, © Good Books, 1992

#19     ***Springs of African Wisdom***, Herder and Herder, 1970

#21     Road Less Traveled, 1983

#24     ***Loving Is*** by Gilbert Hay, Simon & Schuster, Inc., 1967

#25     Bartlett

#30     Haas

#31     M. Gerald Derstine, 1973

#33     ***Tabernacle Hymns***, Tabernacle Publishing Co., 1952

#36     Bartlett

#45     ***A Parent's Bedside Companion*** by Randolph K. Sanders, Herald Press, 1992

#46     Ron Harris Music, 1983

#48-#51 Bartlett

#52     ***Hymnal, A Worship Book***, Brethren Press, Faith & Life Press, Mennonite Publishing House, 1992

#61, #63 Haas

#64     Melody Trails, Inc., 1961 and 1969

#66     ***Songs of Salvation and Service***, Hope Publishing Co., 1923

#67     Bartlett

#71     ***Jubilee Guidebook***, Brethren Press, Evangel Publishing House, Faith & Life Press, Mennonite Publishing House, 1994

#74     Bartlett

#82     ***The Hymnbook***, Hope Publishing Co., 1971

#83     ***For Mature Adults Only*** by Norman C. Habel, Fortress Press, 1969

#84     Haas

#87     Bartlett

#88     ***Love Quotations from the Heart***, Running Press, 1990

#91     ***Many Gifts*** by Patricia Shelly, 1977

#93     Bartlett

#94     ***Assembly Songs*** by Harris J. Loewen, 1983, © Hope Publishing Co.

#96     Haas

#97     ***Thank You Music***, Straightway Music ASCAP, 1977

#100    Bartlett

# The Author

June Galle Krehbiel remembers her childhood, on a farm near Moundridge, Kansas, in vivid detail. Many of these devotionals come from her early memories. Krehbiel remembers her parents reading from the Bible for family devotions before the "always-have-to-have-hot-cereal" breakfasts at the kitchen table. She continued family devotional times and discussions of faith with her own family—husband Perry and children Melanie and Joel.

Krehbiel's education began at the two-room Farms Grade School. She attended Moundridge Elementary School, Moundridge High School, Bethel College (North Newton, Kansas), and the University of Nebraska-Lincoln.

A former elementary and junior high school teacher, Krehbiel has lived with village families in India and taught at a teacher training college in Nigeria. As a freelance writer and college news and publications writer, she loves to fit words together. She enjoys Shasta daisies, church dinners, Kansas skies, ballgames, fat novels, Sunday school, West

African curries, word games, family gatherings, her cat, Alex, and devoted dog, Libby.

Krehbiel has written articles, puzzles, poetry, stories, and book reviews for Mennonite publications. She was a writer for the Jubilee: God's Good News Sunday school curriculum. The family attends Eden Mennonite Church, near Moundridge, where Krehbiel teaches Sunday school.